George Wightman Powers

England and the Reformation, A.D. 1485-1603

George Wightman Powers

England and the Reformation, A.D. 1485-1603

ISBN/EAN: 9783337295585

Printed in Europe, USA, Canada, Australia, Japan

Cover: Foto ©Lupo / pixelio.de

More available books at **www.hansebooks.com**

Oxford Manuals of English History
Edited by C. W. C. OMAN, M.A., F.S.A.

No. IV.

ENGLAND
AND
THE REFORMATION

(A.D. 1485—1603)

BY

G. W. POWERS, M.A.

BARRISTER-AT-LAW, LINCOLN'S INN; SOMETIME SCHOLAR OF NEW COLLEGE

LONDON
BLACKIE & SON, Limited, 50 OLD BAILEY, E.C.
GLASGOW AND DUBLIN
1897

Now in Course of Publication.

THE OXFORD MANUALS
OF ENGLISH HISTORY.

EDITED BY C. W. C. OMAN, M.A., F.S.A.
Fellow of All Souls College, Oxford.

The series will consist of six volumes, bound in neat cloth, with Maps, Genealogies, and Index, price One Shilling each.

I. **The Making of the English Nation**; 55 B.C.-1135 A.D. By C. G. ROBERTSON, B.A., Fellow of All Souls, Modern History Lecturer, Exeter College. [*Ready.*

II. **King and Baronage**; A.D. 1135-1328. By W. H. HUTTON, B.D., Fellow and Tutor of St. John's College. [*Ready.*

III. **The Hundred Years' War**; A.D. 1328-1485. By C. W. C. OMAN, M.A., Editor of the series. [*In preparation.*

IV. **England and the Reformation**; A.D. 1485-1603. By G. W. POWERS, M.A., Late Scholar of New College.
[*Ready.*

V. **King and Parliament**; A.D. 1603-1714. By G. H. WAKELING, M.A., Fellow of Brasenose College. [*Ready.*

VI. **The Making of the British Empire**; A.D. 1714-1832. By A. HASSALL, M.A., Senior Student and Tutor of Christ Church.
[*Ready.*

LONDON
BLACKIE & SON, LIMITED; 50 OLD BAILEY, E.C.
GLASGOW AND DUBLIN

GENERAL PREFACE.

There are so many School Histories of England already in existence, that it may perhaps seem presumptuous on the part of the authors of this series to add six volumes more to the number. But they have their defence: the "Oxford Manuals of English History" are intended to serve a particular purpose. There are several good general histories already in use, and there are a considerable number of scattered 'epochs' or 'periods'. But there seems still to be room for a set of books which shall combine the virtues of both these classes. Schools often wish to take up only a certain portion of the history of England, and find one of the large general histories too bulky for their use. On the other hand, if they employ one of the isolated 'epochs' to which allusion has been made, they find in most cases that there is no succeeding work on the same scale and lines from which the scholar can continue his study and pass on to the next period, without a break in the continuity of his knowledge.

The object of the present series is to provide a set of historical manuals of a convenient size, and at a very moderate price. Each part is complete in itself, but as the volumes will be carefully fitted on to each other, so that the whole form together a single continuous history of England, it will be possible to use any two or more of them in successive terms or years at the option of the instructor. They are kept carefully to the same scale, and the editor has done his best to put before the various authors the necessity of a uniform method of treatment.

The volumes are intended for the use of the middle and upper forms of schools, and presuppose a desire in the scholar to know something of the social and constitutional history of England, as well as of those purely political events which were of old the sole staple of the average school history. The scale of the series does not permit the authors to enter into minute points of detail. There is no space in a volume of 130 pages for a discussion of the locality of Brunanburgh or of the authorship of *Junius*. But due allowance being made for historical perspective, it is hoped that every event or movement of real importance will meet the reader's eye.

All the volumes are written by resident members of the University of Oxford, actively engaged in teaching in the Final School of Modern History, and the authors trust that their experience in working together, and their knowledge of the methods of instruction in it, may be made useful to a larger public by means of this series of manuals.

CONTENTS

CHAP.		Page
I.	Establishment of the Dynasty	7
II.	Henry VIII.: War and Diplomacy	26
III.	The Breach with Rome	42
IV.	The Dictatorship	57
V.	The Minority—Edward VI.	71
VI.	The Reaction—Queen Mary	80
VII.	The Religious Settlement—England, Scotland, and Ireland in Elizabeth's Early Years	88
VIII.	The Struggle with Spain and the Papacy	100
IX.	Conclusion—Elizabeth's Later Years—The Tudor Period	121
	Index	139

Genealogy of Henry VII.	10
Map illustrating English relations with Brittany	13
Genealogy of Charles V.	25
Yorkist Genealogy	27
Plan of Battle of Flodden	30
Plan of Battle of Pinkie	72
Genealogy of the Tudors	137

ENGLAND AND THE REFORMATION

(A.D. 1485 — 1603).

CHAPTER I.

ESTABLISHMENT OF THE DYNASTY, 1485–1509.

The fortunes of England had scarcely ever sunk to a lower point than when the last Plantagenet king perished on the field by Bosworth. All the strength and glory that had distinguished the reigns of Edward I., Edward III., and Henry V. had departed. The extensive dominions which England had so long possessed on the Continent had been utterly lost; Scotland had shaken off every vestige of feudal dependence; and in Ireland the English sway was little more than nominal. Shorn of her empire, and distracted and weakened by thirty years of civil strife, England was no longer of any weight or influence in the affairs of Europe. She had fallen from the roll of great nations; and, in her enfeebled condition, her coasts were assaulted and ravaged with impunity by enemies and pirates, by French, Flemings, and Scots.

Internally, the country presented a scene of disorganisation and decay. The power of the king, which was then the only restraint on the turbulence of the barons, and the only security for peace and order, had been overshadowed by an oligarchy of great nobles, who had accumulated large estates in their hands, and grown richer as the crown had grown poorer. In the face of these "overmyghtye subgettes" all true, sound government had proved impossible. At

Internal state of England in 1485.

the head of military households, or of bands of retainers wearing their livery, they had seized the control of the whole administration, which they thwarted or perverted at their will. The practice of "maintenance" flourished, through which criminals bought or otherwise procured the protection of some lord, who "maintained" their cause and sheltered them from the penalties due to their misdeeds. Sheriffs, and sometimes even judges, were swayed by undue influence, and were guilty of gross partiality in the exercise of their functions; juries were packed, and the jurors bribed or intimidated; and the judicial administration generally was so corrupt and inefficient that the bitter complaint arose that "the law servyth of nowgth ellys but for to do wrong". Private wars and family feuds were common; murders, robberies, and crimes of violence of all kinds were of ordinary occurrence. Laws had been enacted and re-enacted to check the evils that prevailed, but, through the collapse of the royal authority, they could not be enforced, and remained barren and of no effect. The church, which in the troubles of former centuries had been so active in behalf of civilization and order, no longer played its ancient part, but had relinquished its high ideals and seemed buried in helpless lethargy. Intellectually, morally, and materially, the condition of England was "no-wise eligible". Learning had decayed, and its revival in Italy and the South had not yet spread so far north as the British Islands. The increase of superstition and superstitious practices, the belief in and resort to heathenish rites of magic and witchcraft, the dark vices that had characterized the Wars of the Roses, base ingratitude, shameless treachery, revolting cruelty, unredeemed by any noble feeling or sentiment of honour—all were evidence of the moral and spiritual degradation of the nation. Nor was its material condition much better. Foreign and domestic warfare, and frequent outbreaks of pestilence had had their natural effects. The population had diminished. The old social order, based on feudalism, with its rigid and clearly defined 'ranks, had broken up and was fast passing away. The sun of the Middle Ages had set, and the new day had not yet dawned.

The decadence of England was all the more apparent in contrast with the powerful states that were growing up on the Continent. From most humble beginnings the kingdom of France had risen to greatness. By a steady policy of aggrandisement it had absorbed one by one all the great feudal lordships except Brittany, till it extended from the Channel to the Pyrenees, and from the Atlantic to the Alps and the borders of Lorraine. *The Continental Monarchies.* As it expanded externally, it had become more firmly consolidated internally. The nobles, favouring, as in England, the side of disintegration and local independence, had been overthrown by the cunning and persistence of Louis XI., who had built up an absolute power capable of overriding provincial jealousies and welding the different parts of France into a single compact whole. To the south of the Pyrenees a similar process had been taking place. The long, dreary period of disunion, dating from the Muhummadan invasion of the peninsula, was at length drawing to a close. The old rivals, Aragon and Castile, already predominant over the smaller principalities, had by the marriage of Ferdinand and Isabella, their respective rulers, coalesced to form the Spanish monarchy. The advance of the united state was irresistible; and when Ferdinand and Isabella, after putting down internal disturbances, proceeded to attack the remnant of the Moorish kingdom of Granada, the days of the latter were seen to be numbered. In central Europe the Holy Roman Empire still lingered, magnificent in its pretensions, and claiming suzerainty over all lands from the Mediterranean to the Baltic. In the east the Turks, who had captured Constantinople in 1453, were vigorously pushing their conquests and pressing hard on the confines of Hungary. To restore disordered England and place her on an equality with such rival powers, was the heavy task that lay before the victor of Bosworth.

Henry Tudor, Earl of Richmond, could not show a clear and indisputable right to the throne. There were three grounds—descent, conquest, and marriage—on which he might base his claim, but each of them was in some respect faulty or insufficient. By blood he was, on the mother's side, descended from John of Gaunt through the Beaufort line.[1] This line, however, was in its origin illegitimate, and though it had been fully legitimatised by Richard II., it had by a later alteration been expressly barred from the royal dignity. Whether the alteration was valid was indeed open to dispute. But even if no disability rested on the Beauforts, the House of York had, on grounds of descent from Edward III., superior hereditary right, being derived from Lionel, elder brother of John of Gaunt. In this way Henry's title was inferior to that of the children of Edward IV. and of Clarence. He might, however, make out a stronger case for himself by claiming from Henry IV. instead of from Edward III. He was the nearest Lancastrian heir, and could insist that the crown at Henry IV.'s accession had been settled by Parliament on the Lancastrian line, and so had devolved upon him. But this plea, again, was liable to objections. Henry, then, could not clearly establish his right to the kingdom by inheritance. Nor were his other titles more satisfactory. To appeal to conquest would have been galling to English pride, and was in itself somewhat ludicrous; while to appeal to the prospective marriage with Elizabeth, daughter of Edward IV., through which his expedition had

Henry VII.'s claim to the crown: its weakness.

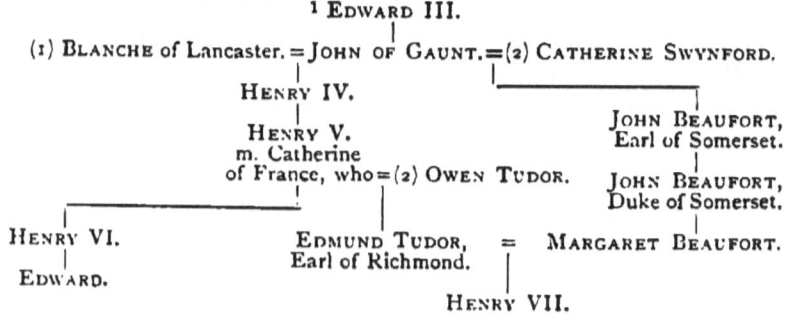

[1] EDWARD III.
(1) BLANCHE of Lancaster.=JOHN OF GAUNT.=(2) CATHERINE SWYNFORD.

HENRY IV.
HENRY V.
m. Catherine
of France, who=(2) OWEN TUDOR.

JOHN BEAUFORT, Earl of Somerset.
JOHN BEAUFORT, Duke of Somerset.

HENRY VI.
EDWARD.

EDMUND TUDOR, Earl of Richmond. = MARGARET BEAUFORT.

HENRY VII.

received Yorkist support and resulted in success, would have been repugnant to his own feeling. Henry of Richmond was as fully determined as afterwards was William of Orange, to be no courtesy king, reigning in right of his wife. For this reason the marriage which effected the union of the two Roses was deferred for five months; nor was Elizabeth crowned as queen till after the revolt of Simnel, which taught Henry the wisdom or necessity of thus conciliating Yorkist sentiment. In reality, the strongest point in favour of Henry was the fact that he was in possession of the throne, and the English nation, thoroughly tired of the dynastic struggle, was willing to accept his rule. Accordingly Parliament, without entering into the question of his legal right, simply declared the crown vested in him and the heirs of his body,—thus covering by its sanction all defects in his title. The settlement thus made was afterwards confirmed by papal bulls.

With the legality of his rule fully established, Henry was in a position to deal more effectively with any opposition. The White Rose was still popular in many districts, especially in the north. Cut off from middle England by a belt of forest, fen, and moorland, which stretched from the Humber and Wash to the estuaries of the Mersey and Dee, the northern counties seemed almost a land apart, and continued still the home of feudal loyalty and spirit. In these parts, particularly in Yorkshire, devotion to Richard III. had been greatest; and in these parts the chief difficulties and troubles of the Tudor monarchs arose. *The discontented Yorkists.* Hoping to win the people to his cause by a personal visit, Henry was in Yorkshire in the spring of 1486, when he was surprised by a hasty rising under Richard's minister, Lord Lovell,—"the dog" of the unfortunate Collingbourn's well-known rhyme, which cost its maker so dear. Lovell hoped by a rapid movement to capture the king, but, failing in this, he fled away, and ultimately escaped to Flanders. There discontented Yorkists found a home at the court of Margaret, widow of Charles the Bold, who, being the sister of Edward

IV., could never forget her Yorkist blood, and was ready to do her utmost for the restoration of her own line. She was "the Juno of Henry", the centre and active support of plots and intrigues against him.

A more alarming attempt followed—the first of those impostures which are characteristic of the time and mark the low intellectual level that prevailed. The youthful Earl of Warwick, son of the false, unstable Clarence, was the nearest male heir of Edward III., and, as a possible danger, had been lodged in the Tower. A rumour that he had been assassinated afforded the basis for an extensive Yorkist conspiracy. Lambert Simnel, son of a joiner or organ-maker of Oxford, was schooled by a priest to personate the captive earl; and suddenly appearing early in 1487 in Ireland, where Yorkist feeling was strong, he was welcomed with acclamation by all classes, and crowned king at Dublin without a voice being raised in Henry's favour. Joined by discontented English, and by a band of German mercenaries sent by Margaret, the pretender landed in Lancashire, trusting to find support in the disaffected north. The king, however, was not caught off his guard. Troops had been already levied, and the real Earl of Warwick had been exhibited in public in order to explode the imposture. The invaders were coldly received even in Yorkshire; and as they made a dash at Newark to secure their entry into the Midlands, they were met at Stoke by the royal forces, and in a short but desperate conflict were entirely cut to pieces (June 16, 1487). The Yorkist leaders all fell in the battle or disappeared,—among them Lovell, and John de la Pole, Earl of Lincoln. The latter was the son of a sister of Richard III., and had been recognised by him as his heir. Lambert himself was captured and pardoned, and was placed in a menial office in the royal kitchen: he had been a mere tool or decoy in a plot which apparently was intended to raise Lincoln to the throne.

Lambert Simnel's imposture. 1487.

Battle of Stoke.

Freed from domestic troubles, Henry was able to direct his attention to continental affairs. The rugged, ironbound land of Brittany, which alone of the great French fiefs had preserved its old independence, was threatened by Charles VIII. and his council, who were bent on completing Louis XI.'s work of centralisation. The opportunity was inviting. Francis, the Breton duke, was weak and incapable, and had, moreover, afforded a fair pretext

for attack by the shelter he was giving to the rebel Duke of Orleans, afterwards Louis XII. In 1487 Charles' troops entered the duchy and laid siege to its chief town, Nantes, which commanded the lower course of the Loire. English feeling was deeply stirred; for Brittany, now that Burgundy had fallen, was England's chief ally on the Continent, and its annexation would give France the possession of an unbroken line of coast facing this country. Henry, however, was too prudent to rush into war blindly and without allies. Being equally bound to the French and Breton courts for succour in his exile, he took up a neutral attitude, seeking to mediate between them, and disavowing the act of Sir Edward Widville, who sailed over with a body of volunteers to the aid of Francis. While Henry allowed himself to be amused by negotiations, the French crushed the Bretons and their English helpers at St. Aubin (July 1488), and dictated peace on their own terms. The unfortunate duke died within a month of his defeat, leaving a daughter, Anne, as his successor. As the new ruler was barely twelve years old, Charles immediately claimed her wardship with other sovereign rights, and invaded the duchy to enforce his demands. The princes most interested in resisting French aggression felt the need of acting without delay, if Brittany was to be saved from absorption. Several thousand English and Spanish troops were sent to assist in its defence; and negotiations for a close league were set on foot between Henry, Ferdinand, and Maximilian, son of the emperor and King of the Romans. But the allies were slow in moving, Maximilian, who was eager to win Anne as his wife, being hampered by a revolt of the Flemings, which was finally put down with English help, and Ferdinand being occupied with his attack on the Moors of Granada. In Brittany, meanwhile, fighting continued, bringing great misery on the inhabitants, who were plundered by both friend and foe. Internal dissensions broke out, and Anne herself alienated some of her most active supporters, without gaining any real strength, by marrying Maximilian by proxy (1490). That prince, ever ready, "like ill archers that draw not their arrows up to the head", to relinquish an object when almost won in favour of some new one, hurried off to make war on Hungary instead of securing his bride and her patrimony. His lack of perseverance was fatal to his interests. The French, pressing their attack, overran the greater part of the duchy; Nantes was delivered up to them by treachery, and Rennes, the town next in importance, had been invested, when Anne, partly from despair and partly from girlish ambition, put an end to the war. Repudiating her unreal union with the King of the Romans, she accepted the hand which Charles

The affairs of Brittany. 1487-90.

offered her, and became his queen (Dec. 1491). Henceforth Brittany from its independent position sank into a province and bulwark of France.

The result of the Breton war was deeply humiliating to English pride, which called for revenge; and in the autumn of 1492, Henry, after waiting in vain for his allies, Ferdinand and Maximilian, crossed over to France with a well-equipped force and assaulted Boulogne. No serious fighting, however, took place or was intended, but at Étaples a treaty was signed (Nov. 1492), by which the English king was to receive an indemnity of 745,000 crowns. *Treaty of Étaples.* Henry, who had obtained from Parliament large grants of money for carrying on hostilities, preferred to further strengthen himself by a lucrative peace. His position was not yet firm enough for active intervention abroad; and Egremont's rising in the north (1489), caused by the levying of a subsidy, had shown how much taxation was hated, and how unwise would be any policy that entailed fresh imposts. Besides, Henry had to cope with a new pretender, who might be dangerous if seconded by French help.

In Ireland, the fertile nursery of political adventurers, a richly-dressed youth had appeared during the preceding winter (1491–92), appealing for help to recover his "just heritage" of England. He gave out that he was Richard, Duke of York, the younger son of Edward IV., and that he had been spared when his brother was murdered in the Tower. In reality he was of burgess origin, a native of Tournai, Perkin Warbeck by name. *Perkin Warbeck in Ireland. 1491.* On the outbreak of war between England and France, he was sent for and honourably entertained by Charles, who hoped to use him as a weapon against Henry. Excluded from France by the Peace of Étaples, the impostor turned to the Low Countries, where he grew into a personage of high importance. Margaret, who was smarting under the failure of her former scheme, acknowledged him as her nephew, "doing him all princely honour, and giving him the delicate title of The White Rose of England". Through her influence the unstable Maximilian and his son, the Archduke Philip, who was the nominal ruler of the Netherlands, were also induced to lend him their countenance. Yorkists and malcontents gradually drew round him; and secret communications were opened with persons of distinction in England. Plans were laid for a great invasion, which was to sweep Henry "a false usurper" from the throne. But the "usurper" was not unaware of the gathering storm. As his remonstrances with the Archduke for allowing Perkin and his fellow-conspirators to remain in Flanders were of no avail, he adopted sharper measures to procure their dismissal. He prohibited all trade with the Flemings, thus cutting off their supply of English wool, which was absolutely indispensable to them as the raw material for their manufactures. Henry also "worked by countermine", sending spies, who obtained for him a knowledge of the conspiracy in all its details. Suddenly, when the plotters were about to strike, he anticipated them by arresting several of their English accomplices and sympathisers.

Execution of William Stanley. 1495. The chief of them were sent to the block, among them his own chamberlain, Sir William Stanley, who had won the fight of Bosworth for him. This prompt action caused the expedition to be postponed; and when in July 1495 it at last sailed and attempted a landing in Kent, it was easily beaten off by the levies of the neighbourhood. All real danger from the impostor was now past, although he continued for more than two years yet to play like a will-o'-the-wisp round the king.

The victory of Bannockburn had given Scotland her independence, but it had wholly failed to secure for her peace and strong governance. Under the weak successors of Robert Bruce the kingly power had sunk almost to nothing. All the evils from which England was suffering in the 15th century were to be found in an exaggerated form north of the Tweed. Fierce and irreconcilably divided among themselves by clannish feuds, the Scots were united only by a blind and deadly hatred of the

English. On the borders between the two kingdoms raids and bloodshed were chronic, and for miles in both directions the land lay untilled and desolate. From the opening of his reign it had been Henry's steady desire to bring about a peace with Scotland, and cement it with a marriage between the royal lines. Such a course would confirm the position of his own dynasty, and also be for the public interest of both nations. But James IV. was too deeply imbued with the Scottish spirit to listen to the advances made to him. He had set his heart on recovering Berwick, and so had sent aid to Warbeck, who, after his miserable failure in Kent, sailed away to Ireland. But that country, under the vigorous rule of Sir Edward Poynings, had ceased to be a happy hunting-ground for Henry's enemies; and, after a vain assault on Waterford, the claimant repaired to the Scottish court. Here he received a royal welcome from James, who treated him as the true Duke of York, and conferred on him in marriage his own relative, the noble and beautiful Catharine Gordon. Nor was James' attitude altered when Philip, under pressure from his subjects, who keenly felt the breach of trade with England, repudiated Warbeck, and concluded the *Intercursus Magnus* with Henry (1496). This, the first great commercial treaty of English history, is also one of the most remarkable. It practically established free-trade between England and Flanders, rejecting the narrow mercantile notions of the age, and anticipating the wiser principles of our own times.

_{Warbeck in Scotland. 1496.}

In the following autumn (1496), James invaded Northumberland in support of his guest's pretensions; but he found the English by no means inclined to stir on Perkin's behalf, and his invasion dwindled into a mere plundering raid. His ill-success inclined him to listen to the advice of Ferdinand and Isabella, who had for some time been urging him to be reconciled with the English king. Charles VIII. had, in 1494, burst into the Italian peninsula, rapidly conquered the kingdom of Naples, and still more rapidly lost it; and the Spanish monarchs were eager to win Henry's adhesion to the league which they formed to exclude the French from Italy. Hence they strove to relieve him of Scottish hostility, that he might be free to act with them on the Continent. It was through their agency that James at length consented to dismiss his guest and sign a truce with Henry. The final act in Perkin's career remained to be played in England itself.

The defence of the northern counties had led to the imposition of a fresh subsidy. The men of Cornwall, a race "stout of stomach and mighty of limb", sprang into revolt against being taxed "for a little stir of the Scots soon blown over". Their chief instigators were Joseph, a blacksmith, "a notable talking fellow", and a lawyer, Flammock, who "spoke learnedly", assuring them that the law was on their side. Refraining from plunder, the rebels swept unopposed across the country towards London, till at Blackheath they were encountered by the king's forces and helplessly mown down by his artillery (June 1497). The introduction of gunpowder was telling in favour of the royal power, the king alone possessing a train of cannon, and thus no longer being at the mercy of an armed mob, as in the days of Tyler and Cade.

<small>Blackheath Field. 1497.</small>

The commotion in the west had not time to settle before Perkin, who had been dismissed from the Scottish court, landed in Cornwall. He was soon at the head of 3000 men, and assuming the title of Richard IV. advanced to seize Exeter. The city gallantly beat off his attacks; and, already disheartened, he lost all courage on the approach of royal troops, and fled away to sanctuary at Beaulieu Abbey in the New Forest. Being induced to surrender and confess his imposture, he was treated with leniency, till, on foolishly trying to escape, he was put in the Tower. There he came into communication with the ill-starred Earl of Warwick—a communication fatal to both. On slight grounds they were accused of conspiring together against the king, and were executed (1499), "this winding-ivy of a Plantagenet thus killing the true tree itself". Warwick's birth was his only offence;

but that was, from a dynastic point of view, an unpardonable one. Yorkist hopes were still so much centred in him that a new impostor had just recently arisen to impersonate him. Besides, his death removed an obstacle to the marriage which Henry was negotiating with the Spanish house. *Execution of Warbeck and Warwick. 1499.*

Friendship with Spain had been the cardinal point of Henry's policy. The French attack on Brittany had first enabled him to draw towards Ferdinand, and to propose a marriage between his son Arthur and the Spanish princess Catharine. Such an alliance was a return to earlier English traditions, and would be a much-needed bulwark to the Tudor throne. But the Spanish king was too cunning to promise his daughter rashly, and the negotiations dragged on for years. Henry, however, was aided in his difficulties by the reputation he enjoyed of being the close ally of Spain, and by actual services which Spain rendered him. Spanish and English troops fought side by side in Brittany; Spanish influence pressed the Archduke Philip to discard Warbeck, and was exercised on Margaret, who at length consented to lay aside her "Junonian" hatred of Henry; and through Spanish diplomacy the truce was brought about between England and Scotland. As the position of Henry improved, Ferdinand showed himself more generously disposed towards the match. He also foresaw the near approach of a struggle between the French king Louis XII., and himself for the sole possession of the Neapolitan kingdom, which they had shamelessly seized and divided between them. In November 1501 the protracted negotiations came to an end, Catharine being sent to England and married to Arthur amid general rejoicing. *The Spanish marriage.*

Henry's success with regard to the Spanish match encouraged him to persevere with the Scottish. He had taken advantage of the truce to move cautiously towards the Scottish king, offering him his eldest daughter Margaret to wife. But James was a person of uncertain temperament, difficult to bind to any definite course of action; and on both sides there were national prejudices to be faced and overcome, the result of two centuries of warfare. Even some of Henry's counsellors are said to have hesitated, fearing that in the failure of male heirs England might fall to the king of Scotland, and become a mere dependency of that country, till they were assured by Henry that the greater would inevitably draw the less, and not the less the greater. Ultimately the king's steady patience and the clever management of his ambassador, Bishop Fox, won the day, and in 1503 at Edinburgh Margaret was wedded to the Scottish king. It was this marriage that was destined in after years to bear as its fruit the final union of Great Britain under one sceptre.

Peace with Scotland.

Since the opening of the reign a great change had taken place in constitutional relations within the realm. The royal authority had been rescued from the low estate to which it had fallen during the century, and over-topping its rivals, was steadily rising into an absolutism. Centralisation was the aim of Henry Tudor, as it had been of Louis XI. of France, and it was pursued by him with similar craft and dissimulation and with similar success. To a large extent circumstances were in his favour. The clergy, frightened by the Lollard movement, clung to the royal power, as their only shield against attack and spoliation; while the people at large longed for a strong government, which would put down disorder and give them protection in their ordinary occupations. With the church and the masses on his side, Henry had only the opposition of the nobles to fear. But the latter had passed the zenith of their influence, and were less powerful in reality than in appearance. The War of the Roses had in fact been fatal to them. They had suffered in prestige far more than in numbers, while their collective might had been weakened by the gaps made in the ranks of their armed retainers. A small group still remained pre-eminent over the rest, and it was against these that the efforts of the Tudors were directed. No opportunity of humili-

Henry's jealousy of the frowning nobles.

ating and destroying them was missed. The temper of Henry VII. expressly fitted him for this task. Like Tiberius of Rome, he had been made by the vicissitudes of his early life watchful, mistrustful, and cruel, "full of thoughts and secret observations, of apprehensions and suspicions". He was a "dark prince", employing as his ministers chiefly clergymen and lawyers, and "keeping a strait hand on his nobility". His execution of Stanley initiated the policy—which characterised the whole dynasty —of striking down at the first breath of disaffection anyone who, from wealth or connections, might be dangerous to the throne.

The legislation of the reign, extensive as it was, was not in any true sense original, and introduced no new principles of law. Its object was to secure the proper execution of the statutes already in existence. The sheriffs and local magistrates were brought under the control of the king and council, and made to enforce the law. In certain cases, where the ordinary tribunals were too weak to deal with offenders, their action was superseded altogether by a special and extraordinary court, created by Act of Parliament in 1487. This court consisted of only seven, afterwards eight members,—all of them ministers or judges,—and was in its origin practically an offshoot from the council. It took cognisance of and enforced the statutes against livery and main- tenance, and other crimes of "force and violence". It retained its separate existence for about fifty years, and, when its work was done, was absorbed again in the council or Star Chamber Court. Another statute, passed in 1495, consolidated Henry's throne by investing him with exceptional powers for coping with attempts against it. It asserted the right of "the king for the time being" to require full and loyal service from his subject in time of rebellion or invasion, and declared that the subject should not be liable to prosecution for acts so done in the cause of the king. Even martial law might be employed with impunity. The government was thus furnished with a sharp weapon with which to smite down discontent.

<small>Livery and Maintenance.</small>

Henry was the first king to perceive and act consistently on the principle that money is power. Warned by the experience of the Lancastrian house, whose weakness and collapse had been largely due to its poverty, he neglected no opportunity of filling his coffers. As taxation was unpopular, the king being expected "to live of his own"—to pay the expenses of his government out of his own revenues,—he fell back on other methods of amassing wealth. Each rebellion was made to bring in a rich harvest: "The less blood he drew, the more he took of treasure". Forced loans were enacted, and 'Benevolences', voluntary or rather involuntary presents, were revived. The levying of a Benevolence for the French war was the occasion on which the chancellor, Archbishop Morton, by whose advice chiefly Henry was guided, is said to have devised the famous dilemma known as "Morton's fork" or "crutch". The collectors were to press the frugal to contribute on the ground of their frugality, which showed that they were saving, and the luxurious on the ground of their luxury, which showed that they had enough and to spare. "So neither kind came amiss."

The king's hoard.

The rigid execution of the laws was a source of profit to the king, whose arm could now reach the mightiest. The Earl of Oxford, Admiral of England, was Henry's "principal servant both for war and peace". On one occasion, to do honour to the king who was his guest, he drew up his servants "in their livery coats with cognizances" or badges. Henry thanked him for the compliment, but would not tolerate a breach of law, even by his chief and most faithful subject. "By my faith, my lord, I thank you for my good cheer, but I may not endure to have my laws broken in my sight: my attorney must speak with you." The result of the interview was a fine of 15,000 marks for the royal exchequer

Necessary as the enforcement of law was, it was carried to excess and abused. The legal system was strained for the sake of fines: obsolete statutes were raked up, royal feudal rights pressed to the utmost, and informers and accusations encouraged. Henry's chief agents in this work, "his horse-leeches and shearers", were two lawyers, Empson and Dudley, who, at the beginning of the next reign, suffered death for their zeal in his service. With increasing years the love of money, as is usual, grew upon him, and deepened into avarice. He left in his treasury £1,800,000, a sum equivalent to ten times that amount to-day. In spite of his greed he was no miser; he was fond of fine clothes and fine palaces. His wealth rendered him still more absolute, making him independent of Parliament, which met only once during the last twelve years of his reign.

Empson and Dudley.

After Warwick's execution no rebellion occurred to trouble Henry. He had beaten down faction wherever it showed itself, and was henceforth free to strengthen his throne at home, and raise its status in the eyes of Europe. In the alliance with Spain he had been the inferior and obliged party, and he invariably touched his bonnet when the names of Ferdinand and Isabella were mentioned. It was his ambition to place himself on terms of equality with those monarchs. Arthur, who was a youth of studious habits and weak health, died shortly after his marriage. Squabbles at once arose respecting Catharine's dowry, Ferdinand and Henry alike being close-fisted and higgling with one another like two Jews. In the end the matter was settled by an agreement that the young widow should be married to Prince Henry, the brother of Arthur; and a papal dispensation was obtained to authorise the union of persons so closely connected. The Spanish alliance was too valuable for Henry to give up altogether, but he made no haste to carry out the new arrangement. Having possession of Catharine, he was in a position to wait, and to force his own terms on the Most Catholic King.

Marriage of Prince Henry and Catharine of Aragon.

He was himself a candidate in search of a fitting wife. His queen, Elizabeth, towards whom he "was nothing uxorious", and whose liveliness must have accorded ill with his gravity, had died early in 1503. Although nearly worn out, Henry indulged like an inconstant youth in successive projects of marriage, which give an almost comic colouring to his later years. In each case his wooing was directed solely by his thirst for power or wealth. (1) At first he thought of the young Queen of Naples; but, though most beautiful and accomplished, she lacked the one thing needful—a tempting dowry. (2) Margaret, sister of the Archduke Philip, was a far more attractive match. Already twice married, she had been endowed with rich grants of property by both her husbands. In addition she was left in command of the wealthy, commercial Low Countries by her brother, when he set out to assume the government of Castile, which had by strict law descended to his wife Juana on the death of her mother Isabella in November 1504. Henry was already negotiating for a union with Margaret, when fortune threw in his path a happy chance on which he was not slow to fasten. While the archduke passed down the Channel on his way to Spain, he was driven by a storm into Weymouth harbour, and, being splendidly entertained by the English king, was induced to conclude a treaty with him, by which he promised to give him his sister Margaret to wife, and to surrender the Earl of Suffolk, an English exile in the Netherlands. Suffolk was naturally an object of fear to Henry, being the next brother of the Earl of Lincoln killed at Stoke, and so the representative of Yorkist claims. He was actually delivered up by Philip, and was put to death, it is said by Henry's instructions, early in the succeeding reign. But the other half of the treaty was not so easy of execution, Margaret offering a lively opposition to the arrangement made for her. She was only about twenty-seven years old, and had no mind to be married to a prince whose age was nearly double her own.

Fate of the De la Poles.

(3) A new prospect was opened out by the death of the archduke, which occurred soon after his arrival in Spain. His widow Juana was insane, but as her hand carried with it the important kingdom of Castile, Henry

offered to marry her in spite of her madness. Ferdinand naturally objected, both as father of the lady and as ruler of Castile, which he had no desire to part with. After persisting for some time, the English suitor was convinced of the hopelessness of his project, and turned back towards Margaret and the house of Maximilian, now emperor. The Hapsburgs were evidently destined to a brilliant future, for Charles, the young grandson of the emperor, besides inheriting the Netherlands, would one day succeed to all the Spanish dominions.[1] Henry purposed to ally himself with the rising house by two marriages, one between himself and Margaret, and the other between his daughter Mary and Prince Charles. The latter match was, through a timely present of money to the needy emperor, actually arranged (1508): not so that of Henry himself. Margaret was too independent to be coerced, and Henry died a widower (April 1509). His later diplomacy, restless as the ocean, had been almost as unfruitful. It had produced more alarm to Ferdinand than solid advantage to his own kingdom. That monarch, being of Aragonese blood, was obnoxious to the proud Castilians, and had felt his position in Castile threatened by the growing connection between Henry, Maximilian, and Charles. He had thus been led to make some concessions respecting Catharine's dowry and to agree to pay it before the marriage with Prince Henry was celebrated.

More Spanish marriage schemes.

[1] GENEALOGY OF CHARLES V.

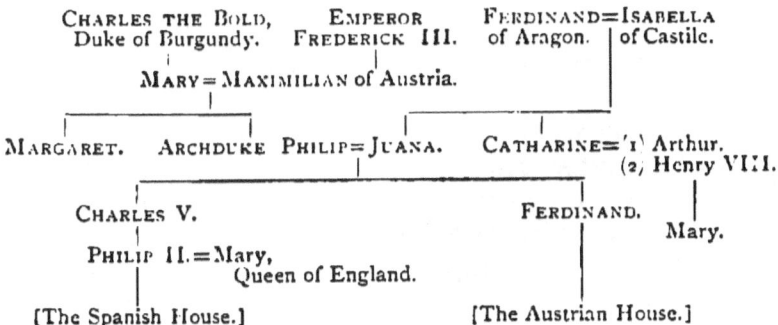

Suspicious and cruel, acute and successful, avaricious and yet not without magnificence, the first Tudor king remains unloved and unlovable. In temperament he was scarcely English,—a formidable man who had no pleasures; and he never enjoyed any degree of popularity. Whether he was really a great king is open to question: the greatness of the reign in its results is beyond dispute. England was saved from the dissolution that had threatened to overwhelm her; the anarchy was ended, and a centralised system of government established, capable of enforcing law and order. Commerce grew, Henry studiously encouraging it and giving help to John and Sebastian Cabot, who discovered Newfoundland and sailed along the North American coast. The reign had also coincided with a critical epoch in the world's history. The rule of the Crescent had been swept from Western Europe; Vasco da Gama had doubled the Cape of Good Hope and opened the sea-route to India and the East (1497–98); a native of Genoa, Christopher Columbus, had crossed the Atlantic and discovered the western world (1492). On all sides the horizon of Christendom was widening; while the Renaissance, or Revival of Learning, stimulated by the recent discovery of printing, was advancing irresistibly across the face of Europe. The middle ages were vanishing, and unmistakable signs heralded the advent of a new era.

Character of Henry.

CHAPTER II.

HENRY VIII.: WAR AND DIPLOMACY. 1509–1530.

The descent of Charles VIII. into Italy (1494) had shown the utter disunion of the peninsula and its helplessness before external attack. It had rudely broken a spell, and henceforward Italy was a prey to be struggled for between the compact nations that surrounded it. Louis XII. made good his claim to the Milanese, while

THE YORKIST FAMILIES.

YORKIST GENEALOGY.

Showing possible claimants to the throne under the Tudors.

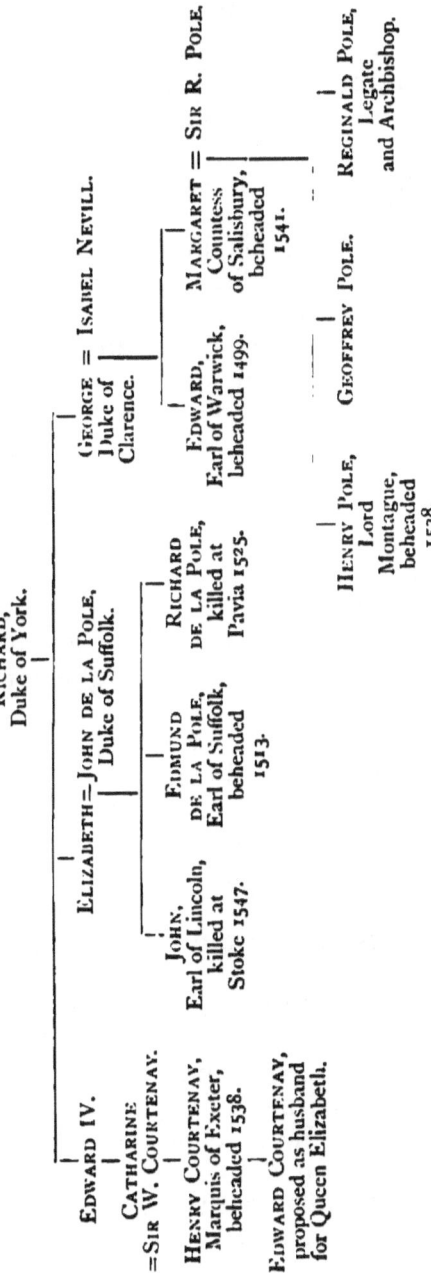

Ferdinand possessed himself of the kingdom of Naples. Julius II., who ascended the pontifical throne in 1503, was a warrior rather than a priest, and was determined at any cost to extend the papal dominions. The first great obstacle to his schemes was Venice, the most powerful of the Italian states, and at his instigation the League of Cambrai sprang up (1508) between France, Spain, the empire, and the papacy, for the dismemberment and spoliation of that republic. The chief result of the war was a large increase of French power in Italy, and so the pope, before the Venetian state had been entirely destroyed, broke up the confederacy which he had himself formed, and began hostilities with the French to the cry of "Out with the barbarians". Louis retaliated by attacking Julius on his ecclesiastical side, and by causing an anti-papal council to be summoned at Pisa. The pontiff, exclaiming that the church was in danger, appealed to all Christian princes for help against "the son of iniquity"; and in October 1511 Spain and Venice combined with him in the Holy League for the defence of the Papal See.

Foreign affairs at accession of Henry VIII.

The appeal of Julius was not lost on the young English king. Uniting in himself the families of Lancaster and York, Henry seemed to have no reason, like his predecessor, for dreading the recurrence of civil war. Handsome, athletic, accomplished, with frank open-handed manners, and a passion for outdoor sports, he was the object of an enthusiastic loyalty which throughout his life was never entirely withdrawn from him. He had increased his popularity by causing Empson and Dudley to be put to death for their extortions, and had carried out the arrangement made by his father by marrying Catharine. Eager to win distinction abroad, and fired by the idea of being the champion of the pope, Henry acceded to the Holy League. Trusting in his first campaign to the experienced guidance of his father-in-law, Ferdinand, he sent troops (1512) to co-operate with him for the recovery of Guienne; but the

Early policy of Henry VIII.

Spanish king, paying no heed to his engagements, occupied himself with seizing Navarre, till the English soldiers broke out into mutiny, and in violation of their orders returned home. The failure was galling, but it was more than counterbalanced by the reverses of the French in Italy, and by the adhesion of Maximilian to the league. In the next summer, after an indecisive engagement between the French and English fleets, Henry crossed to Calais to invade France from the side of the Netherlands. His pride was flattered by the Emperor Maximilian joining him as a volunteer and accepting his pay. The town of Térouanne was invested, and an attempt to relieve it brought on an encounter near Guinegate, which from the sudden panic and flight of the French knights received the name of the Battle of the Spurs. This easy victory of the English was followed by the surrender of Térouanne, and by the capture of the more important fortress of Tournai. Invasion of France. 1513.

Meanwhile French influence had succeeded in breaking the alliance which Henry VII. had formed with so much difficulty between England and Scotland; and, as in the year of Creci, the French war brought a Scotch war in its train. Minor differences had arisen between the two countries from occurrences on the borders, and from the capture and execution of the Scottish sailor Barton as a pirate, but these James had agreed to submit to arbitration. The opportunity afforded by Henry's absence on the Continent was, however, too tempting for him to resist. Listening to the representations of Louis he passed the Tweed with a numerous army, and took up a strong position on Flodden Edge, but only to display his incapacity as a general. Without offering any opposition he allowed the English commander, the wary Earl of Surrey, to sweep round his flank, cross the Till, and sever him from Scotland. Being thus compelled to fight he moved down from the higher ground, and on Flodden Field his army was cut to pieces, he himself and the flower of his nobility being amongst the slain (September 1513). [See plan on next page.] Flodden Field. 1513.

With Scotland crippled Henry looked for a decisive attack on France. But his allies, Ferdinand and Maximilian, having attained their own objects, basely deserted him, and made a truce with Louis. The "Most Catholic

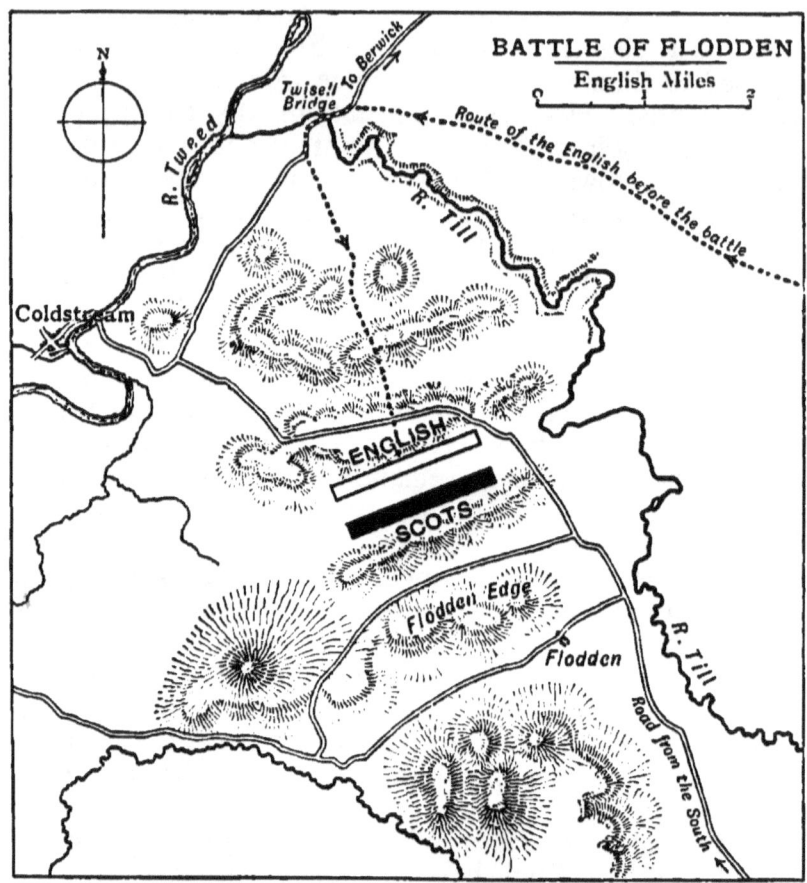

King" in particular was more self-seeking and suspicious than ever. In his miserable jealousy he intrigued with the emperor to break off the match which had been negotiated in the last reign for their common grandson Charles with the English Princess Mary. It seemed that England would be left isolated, when by a sudden move the schemers were anticipated in their plans, Henry, who had already spent his father's hoards in pageantry and war, forming a close alliance with the French king, and transferring to him Mary's hand in marriage (1514). By thus taking a course of her own England asserted her independence of action, and threw off Spanish patronage, under which she had entered the arena of European politics.

The French treaty was the work of Thomas Wolsey. The son of a respectable trader of Ipswich, Wolsey had been educated for the priesthood, and at Oxford had won the title of "The Boy Bachelor" through the early age at which he obtained his degree. Introduced to business of state by Fox, Bishop of Winchester, he at once distinguished himself by his ability and despatch. His untiring zeal in the preparation of supplies for the war, and his skill in negotiating the alliance with France, won for him the first place in the young king's favour. *Rise of Wolsey.* For the next fifteen years he was chief minister of the crown without a rival. Honours and ecclesiastical preferments were showered upon him; in quick succession he became Archbishop of York, Bishop of Winchester, Chancellor, Cardinal, and Papal Legate; and he aspired to the papacy itself. His establishment and style of living were princely, and of him the Venetian ambassador could write: "This man is seven times greater than the pope himself".

The war had convinced Wolsey of the inefficacy of English military action on the Continent. He perceived, and was the first to perceive, the advantages of the insular position of this country, and that more might be gained by diplomacy, by holding the balance between contending powers and preventing any one from becoming supreme, than by war. His policy, in so far as it was his own, seems to have been inspired by this idea. As he was the last of the series of great ecclesiastical statesmen which had begun with Dunstan, so he was the first of a line of great English diplomatists.

In January 1515 Louis XII. died. A valetudinarian of fifty-three, he had in vain tried to respond to the gaieties of his sprightly wife, who was still in her teens, and perished under the change effected in his dinner-hour and the revolution in his habits. Mary, who did not mean to be again used as a pawn in her brother's diplomatic game, at once wedded her old lover, Charles Brandon, Duke of Suffolk. The close connection just established between England and France was already at an end, when Francis I., the new French king, invaded Italy, announcing that he would make "the monarchy of Christendom rest under the banner of France as it was wont to do". At Marignano, near Milan, after a "giant-like" conflict of two days, he defeated the Swiss, who had hitherto been regarded as invincible. Fear of French predominance, together with jealousy of Francis, who was his rival in personal accomplishments and grace, impelled Henry to intervene. But he was without sure allies, and his late experience disinclined him to active hostilities. Indirect means were resorted to, subsidies being furnished to the emperor and the Swiss to attack the French in Lombardy.

Meanwhile French ambition was equally active in Scotland. After Flodden, that kingdom had lain helpless before Henry, but he had forborne to press his victory, trusting to his sister Margaret and the English party to quietly bring about a renewal of friendship with England. Margaret, however, proved unequal to the task. Her marriage with Douglas, Earl of Angus, and her favouritism towards his kinsfolk, roused the jealous temper of the Scots, so that when the Duke of Albany, with the connivance and support of Francis, landed in the country, he had little difficulty in overthrowing her and getting possession of the regency. This triumph of French influence was naturally irritating to the English king, who had recourse to counter-intrigues in order to neutralise it. The whole position was threatening and uncertain, but Wolsey skilfully avoided an open breach, and after patient negotiations drew up the Treaty of London with Francis (October 1518). Albany was excluded for a space from Scotland,

Henry's Scottish policy.

and in exchange for 600,000 crowns, Henry's conquest, Tournai, was to be restored to France. The King of Spain, the emperor, and Pope Leo X. afterwards acceded to the compact, and thus through the initiative of England a universal peace again reigned among the nations of Europe.

The Treaty of London was in harmony with the new principle of the Balance of Power—a principle which originated in Italy to regulate the mutual relations of the different Italian powers, and which spread in the early years of the sixteenth century to international relations in general. No one state was left predominant in Europe. France, indeed, had acquired the Milanese, but her aggressive schemes in Scotland had been cut short, and, more over, she was face to face with a power as formidable as herself. Charles had by will inherited the dominions of his grandfather Ferdinand; and his empire embraced Naples and the Netherlands, Spain and the Spanish possessions in the New World. *The vacancy in the Empire. Charles V. elected.* His growing importance was viewed with dislike by the French king, who, on the death of Maximilian (January 1519), came forward to compete with him for the crown of the Cæsars. Money was so profusely lavished by both monarchs on the electors that to an impartial eye-witness the empire appeared "the most dearest merchandise that ever was sold". Henry himself was caught by the glamour of the vacant office, and purposed to become a third candidate "as being of the Germany tongue". His resolve, however, came too late, and in June 1519 the Spanish monarch was elected emperor, as Charles V.

Francis, with his high spirit, was not the man to tamely acquiesce in the victory of his rival. Already there were outstanding difficulties and disputes between them at almost every point where their territories met. These, aggravated by personal jealousy, made a conflict sooner or later inevitable, and each in anticipation of it turned to secure the alliance of England. But Wolsey, who was now Cardinal-Legate and at the height of his fortune, was fully alive to the advantages of neutrality and to the danger of making either of the rivals supreme. It was his aim to skilfully make use of their antagonism to enhance the importance of England and of her alliance. Hence when Francis requested an interview with Henry in order to win him over to his side, the Cardinal at the same time arranged a counter-interview between Henry and the emperor. In June 1520, outside Calais, between Guisnes and Ardres, the English and French monarchs met amid a scene of splendour and magnificence that won for the place of meeting the name of "The Field of the Cloth of Gold". Many of the nobles were said "to wear their mills, forests, and meadows on their backs". The interview, however, had no political result such as Francis had hoped for. Before leaving home Henry had received an informal visit from the emperor, whom he in turn visited at Gravelines, and with whom he signed a treaty preventing the two opponents from coming to terms to the disadvantage of England.

The Field of the Cloth of Gold. 1520.

The diplomatic contest was still proceeding when in the following year (1521) the expected hostilities broke out. Henry, as the friend of both sides, made a formal offer of mediation, which was accepted. None of the three monarchs, however, had any real desire for peace, and the conference, which assembled at Calais for the settlement of the dispute, was false and hollow from the beginning. Under cover of it Henry entered into a league with the emperor, who, being hampered by a revolt in Spain and by the religious troubles in Germany consequent on Luther's protest, was prepared to bid the higher price for his support. He bound himself to marry Henry's infant daughter Mary, to make good the sums due to him from the French, and to co-operate in a campaign for the recovery of the old Plantagenet possessions across the Channel.

In October 1522 Surrey, son of the hero of Flodden, entered Picardy at the head of an English force; but few imperialists joined him, and beyond useless ravages nothing was effected or even attempted. Each of the confederates blamed the other for the ill-success, but their mutual recriminations were hushed when the Duke of Bourbon, constable and chief noble of France, deserted to them. His defection was held to fore- *Suffolk's Invasion of France. 1523.* shadow many others, so that the English king began to dream of becoming a second Henry of Monmouth and of driving Francis from his throne. Plans were laid for a simultaneous advance on Paris from three different quarters, but his ally again failed him, while his own fine army led by Suffolk, after marching southwards as far as Montdidier, mutinied (1523). All too late the king recognised the cold, selfish nature of Charles V., and withdrew for the time from any direct part in the war.

Such a withdrawal was necessary on other grounds. The old trouble with Scotland had again revived. As soon as war had threatened, Albany had returned to that country, where his presence soon made French influence supreme. The Scotch lords swore to stand by him to the death, and a rupture with England inevitably followed. The district south of the Cheviots, left bare of troops by the French expedition, lay at Albany's mercy, but, being no soldier, he was deceived by the blustering tone assumed by Lord Dacre and enticed into a truce (1522). The danger was averted for the moment, and in all haste Surrey was hurried from Picardy to command against the Scots, whom he punished by a series of merciless raids. Receiving fresh reinforcements from France, Albany in the closing months of 1523 again moved southwards, but, finding the English general prepared to meet him, he retired. It was evident that he was merely waiting for an opportunity to strike, and that the absence of the English army abroad would be the signal for an invasion of the northern shires.

Besides ruining Henry's scheme of peaceably attaching Scotland to himself, the French war had also, through the taxation it entailed, brought him into difficulties with his subjects. Hitherto nothing had occurred to disturb his popularity. He was obeyed as no king had been before him. Under him the court, reflecting the influence of the Renaissance, became splendid and brilliant, and its gorgeous masques and pageants still further impressed the people with a sense of the king's majesty. But Henry, while inheriting from his mother the Yorkist fondness for grandeur and profusion, had at the same time all his father's love of power. He was determined that there should be no will or authority that could interfere with or thwart his own. Besides giving a close attention to affairs of state himself, he was careful to follow his predecessor's example and exclude great nobles from posts of importance. His trusted agents and councillors were, like the Cardinal, men of the middle classes, who, owing everything to the royal favour, in turn worked to magnify and exalt the royal prerogative. On the new class of officials the old aristocracy looked with scorn and hatred, watching for a chance to overthrow them and regain their own lost influence. Of these feelings the Duke of Buckingham made himself the representative and mouthpiece. Son of the duke who had perished under Richard III., he was one of the wealthiest of the peers, and was connected with the Nevills, Percies, and all the chief houses of England. His discontent, which he was too haughty and passionate to hide, was all the more threatening in view of his descent and the state of the royal succession. Sprung from John of Gaunt through the Beaufort line, he regarded himself, in the absence of any male issue to Henry, as the next heir to the throne. Rashly listening to the prophecies of a crazy monk that he would one day be king, he was arraigned for treason, condemned, and executed (May 1521). The fall of the leading man of their order was a sharp warning to the nobles not to cross the path of the king.

Execution of Buckingham. 1521.

The nation at large was indifferent to the humiliation of the baronial families, but it was keenly sensitive to an increase of taxation. While the peace lasted, the ordinary revenue of the crown, eked out by payments from Francis, had through Wolsey's able management proved quite sufficient; there had been no need to resort to Parliament for supplies; and since 1515 the Houses had never met. It seemed as if under the new régime the national assembly of England were destined to suffer the fate of the States-General of France. The royal power would then be left without a check. The war, however, by the heavy military expenditure which it caused, broke down the finances; and an appeal to the nation for help became inevitable. In April 1523 Parliament assembled, and was required to vote the sum of £800,000, to be raised by an impost of 4s. in the pound on all lands and goods. Though the war with France was popular, a fierce opposition at once blazed up, "so that the House was like to have been dissevered". The Cardinal argued, bullied, terrorised; and in the end, through his efforts, seconded by the "faithful diligence" of Sir Thomas More, who had been appointed Speaker by the favour of the court and who warmly supported the court's demands, most of the sum proposed was actually voted, but the payment of it was to be spread over a period of four years.

The futile enterprise of Suffolk in the following autumn (1523) left the royal exchequer more embarrassed than ever; but, after the recent experience, another appeal for the "loving contributions" of Parliament was out of the question. The only course open seemed to be to conclude peace, and to conclude it on terms of an indemnity to England. Wolsey had begun cautiously to feel his way in this direction when tidings came of the total defeat and capture of Francis at Pavia (Feb. 1525). All the martial ardour of the English king returned; his face had "beamed with delight" at the news; and he again resumed his overtures to his ally Charles for a joint invasion of France. Money had to be raised in some way. As Henry proposed to take part in the expedition himself, the Cardinal, making use of a feudal notion that had long been obsolete, demanded a special contribution or aid towards the royal expenses. Under the fair name of an "amicable loan" subjects were called on to furnish one-sixth of the assessed value of their property to the king. The real amicableness of the loan was soon apparent. The subsidy granted by Parliament had not yet been wholly paid, and on the new demand supervening "the people spake cursedly", while in Suffolk and the eastern counties, which were suffering acutely from an agrarian crisis and from depression of the cloth-making trade, riots and tumults broke out. So ominous were the signs of discontent that the idea of a loan based on a fixed assessment was given up, and an ordinary benevolence was resorted to in its stead. The result was not altogether satisfactory to the royal treasury.

The emperor meanwhile was pursuing his own course regardless of his ally. No imperial pride restrained him from borrowing and spending Henry's money, but he was determined that none of the spoils of victory should fall to Henry's lot. His policy throughout was marked by the most mean and studied selfishness. He had solemnly engaged to support Wolsey's election to the papacy, on which the English king declared that he had set his heart, but although the apostolic chair had been twice vacant in the space of two years (1521-23), he had on each occasion been false to his word, and had successively promoted the election of Adrian VI. and Clement VII., both of them prelates whom he considered subservient to his interests. He was now intriguing to keep Henry and Francis asunder, in order to extort from the latter the highest possible terms for himself. The English monarch had good reason to be angry at the duplicity and shabbiness of his "good-brother"; and in the autumn of 1525, listening to Wolsey's advice, he concluded a treaty with France, by which he was to receive 2,000,000 crowns in annual instalments.

<small>Breach with the Emperor. 1525.</small>

His change of attitude was more important than as merely suiting his monetary needs. It brought with it peace with Scotland, which generally followed the lead of France, and so gave a respite to the irritating and exhausting struggle on the borders. It also helped to restore the equilibrium of power in Europe, which had been disturbed by Charles' overthrow of the French and annexation of the rich district of Lombardy. Opposition to him was encouraged, the Italian states with Pope Clement VII. combining together against him. At the same time he was checked by the social and religious tumults in Germany, and by the great victory of the Turks over the Hungarians at Mohats (1526). Before these difficulties his dream of a universal monarchy, which had seemed so near on the morrow of Pavia, faded away. The Italian league however went down before him, and its collapse led in April 1527 to a formal alliance between Henry and Francis, the latter answering for the emperor's debts to Henry and betrothing his second son to Henry's daughter Mary.

So far the chief interest of the reign had lain in its foreign relations. Though much of the diplomacy had been tortuous and barren, yet the general result had been to raise England out of the obscurity and neglect into which she had fallen in the previous century, and vindicate her position as one of the great powers of Europe by the side of France and Spain. Such had been the work of Henry and his minister Wolsey. Henceforward the centre of interest began to shift to home affairs, where events were impending that were destined to vitally affect the whole later history of the country.

During the summer of 1527 it became known that Henry was questioning the validity of his marriage with Catharine. According to the ideas of the time there was nothing surprising in his wish to be separated from her. The frequent use of papal dispensations had impaired the sanctity of wedlock, and marriages were both made and unmade for purely political reasons. When a boy Henry had been betrothed to his queen, who was five and a half years his senior, merely to suit his father's policy and preserve the connection with Spain. That connection was now being dissolved, and Catharine, who regarded herself as its guardian, did not trouble to hide her displeasure at the fact. Moreover, the shadow of the civil war had not yet passed away

The divorce question broached.

from the land, and the folly of Buckingham appeared to show that, if Henry died without a son and heir, the storm would again burst forth. To ensure the peaceful descent of the crown legitimate male offspring to the king was required, but none existed. Of several children only one, a daughter, survived, and as the queen was sickly and prematurely aged, Henry's only hope of the son he ardently desired lay in second nuptials.

His first impulse was simply to declare his marriage null and void from the beginning, as having been contracted with a brother's widow; but it had been sanctioned by a dispensation of Julius II., and so Henry based his claim to be free of Catharine on the plea that the dispensation itself was faulty, irregular, and invalid. To test the question a preliminary action was begun in Wolsey's legatine court; but this was soon dropped, and it remained to submit the matter to the Pope. A former pontiff had divorced Louis XII. in order that he might marry Anne of Brittany, and so secure that province for his crown. Henry's case was far stronger, but with it powerful political interests were involved. Catharine was aunt to the emperor, and not only did she defend her rights with all the spirit of her race, but her cause was also warmly espoused by her nephew, who was determined at all costs to maintain his influence in England. In May 1527 his troops under Bourbon stormed and brutally sacked Rome, and Pope Clement became a prisoner in his hands. To counteract this advantage and win the co-operation of Francis in "the king's matter", as Henry's suit was termed, Wolsey crossed the Channel and drew closer the league with France.

In the meantime Henry's fancy had been caught by Anne Boleyn, a lady of his court and niece to the Duke of Norfolk, a lively brunette, with fascinating eyes and wondrous flowing black hair. His infatuation made him impatient for a favourable verdict in his suit; but a favour-
Rise of Anne Boleyn. able verdict could not be expected at Rome, where the emperor's word was law. Wolsey's secretary, the acute Stephen Gardiner, was sent as envoy

to Italy. By him Clement was induced to issue a commission to two legates, Wolsey and Campeggio, to try the case in London, but he obstinately refused to grant them absolute powers, so that any verdict they gave would still need ratification by himself. In truth the pope was, as between Henry and Charles, "between the hammer and the anvil". His only idea was to temporise to the utmost and use the opportunity to regain some of his power.

Campeggio carried out the policy of procrastination to the letter. He delayed alike on his journey and after his arrival in England. He was confirmed in so acting by the favour with which the cause of Catharine and the Spanish connection was regarded among Englishmen. Rumours, too, came of a brief of Julius, said to make good all flaws and defects in the dispensation. It was not till June 1529 that the trial actually began before the legates in the Black Friars' Hall. Both Henry and Catharine were cited; and the spectacle of the English king pleading before a papal tribunal gave a shock to the national sentiment, and smoothed the way for the approaching abolition of the papal supremacy. Catharine denied the court's jurisdiction and appealed to Rome. The proceedings dragged on, but were an empty show, for the pope had already secretly promised the emperor to break up the trial. In August the Peace *Campeggio's* of Cambrai between France and Spain left *abortive mission.* Charles undisputed master in Italy. Clement abrogated the commission of Wolsey and Campeggio, and called back the suit for his own hearing. "The Vicar of Christ" was merely the emperor's servant; a decision adverse to Henry was only a question of time.

Henry fumed at this, his first failure, and it was on Wolsey, whom he held accountable for it, that his wrath fell. The great cardinal had few friends and many enemies. He was disliked by the ecclesiastical party for his religious reforms and by the reformers for his conservatism. The nobles hated him as an upstart, the people as the cause of the "sore" taxation. Depending solely on the royal favour, that favour was now lost to him. At the lords' prompting an accusation was laid against him by the king, for having broken Richard II.'s Statute of Præmunire by accepting and exercising the legatine authority within the realm. Submitting himself absolutely to Henry's pleasure, he was stripped of his office and goods and exiled to his diocese of York, which he had never yet visited.

<small>Wolsey disgraced.</small>

But his foes, at whose head was Norfolk, were not satisfied. The sense of their own inferiority and the news of the popularity he was gaining in the north by the discharge of his neglected archiepiscopal duties made them fear his possible return to power. An Italian physician, Agostino, was bribed to act as informer against him, and "sang the tune as they wished him". Some communications, which Wolsey indiscreetly held with the French and imperial envoys, were used to whet Henry's anger against him. Arrested on a charge of high treason, he utterly broke in spirit; his health, which had never been strong, collapsed; and on November 29th, 1530, he expired at Leicester Abbey, protesting to the last his faithful service to the king.

<small>Death of Wolsey. 1530.</small>

CHAPTER III.

THE BREACH WITH ROME (1529-35).

Already, before the death of Wolsey, the king and Parliament had taken in hand the question of ecclesiastical reform. For a century and a half the general condition of the church of Western Christendom had been anything but satisfactory. Throughout the clerical body, from the pope and papal court downwards, grave abuses existed: the phrase ran that "the church was corrupt in head and members". Attempts to provide a remedy had already been made by the Councils of Constance and Basel, but had ended in failure. Of three recent popes, Alexander VI. had been an un-

<small>Corruption of the Papacy.</small>

blushing profligate, Julius II. a ruthless warrior, and Leo X. a polished agnostic, who is said to have termed Christianity "a profitable fable". When such was the character of the head of the church, the state of the church under him could scarcely be other than lamentable. Reform was a necessity; and as joint or common action had proved to be impossible, different nations were now to take up the question for themselves.

In this country there had been numerous signs and warnings of the approaching change. The national sentiment had been again and again outraged by the aggressions of the Roman see on the liberties of England and the English Church. It had inspired the enactment of Statutes of Præmunire and Provisors to check the pope's exercise of jurisdiction within the realm, and to prevent him from robbing ecclesiastical patrons of their rights. The constant outflow of money to the Roman treasury had been the subject of repeated complaints. But discontent was not confined to the external relations of the English Church: it existed also in regard to its internal condition. Wyclif had attacked the clergy as rich, worldly, and corrupt; and the effect of his attack had never died away. Lollardy, though extinguished as a political force, still survived in the form of deep, if latent, dissatisfaction at ecclesiastical abuses. Those abuses were neither imaginary nor trivial. *Ancient dislike of Rome in England.* Gascoigne, a chancellor of the University of Oxford and a man of unblemished orthodoxy, has left almost as black a picture of the church's condition as the great Lollard himself. In his *Book of Truths*, written in the middle of the fifteenth century, he specifies seven chief sources of corruption, "rivers of Babylon". Unfit and unworthy persons were ordained and received preferment; bishops and clergy lived away from their cures, so that neglect of spiritual duties was general and preaching rare; pluralities abounded; tithes were impropriated or "stolen" from the parishes, particularly by monasteries; absolution was lightly given or even sold; papal indulgences were hawked about, and were rapidly destroying all morality; papal licenses and dispensations had become a flagrant abuse. Gascoigne does not spare the degraded papacy, but boldly condemns Rome as "the principal wild beast that has laid waste the vineyard of the church".

A general laxity seems to have pervaded the ecclesiastical body. In all sections of it, upper or lower, secular or monastic, there was a similar want of energy and vitality. Duties were inadequately attended to or ignored altogether. This was notably the case with bishops, who were often, like Morton or Wolsey, entirely absorbed in political business. Yet, in spite of their deficiencies, the clergy were a highly privileged class. Their wealth was beyond all question. They had, in the face of mortmain statutes, made themselves masters of a large part of the land of the country, amounting perhaps to one-fifth or even one-fourth of the whole. In Parliament, after the Civil War, they had the majority in the Upper House, which was then the more important one of the two. In addition to this they possessed in Convocation a separate legislature, and in the ecclesiastical courts a separate judicature of their own, the latter being independent of the king and centred in the pope, to whom the ultimate appeal lay. They thus formed within the state a kind of *imperium in imperio*. Their judicial power was the most valued of their privileges. They still retained the substance of what Becket had won for them by his death. In general the clerical courts alone could try "ecclesiastical persons", who were, in virtue of "benefit of clergy", exempt from the ordinary jurisdiction of the realm, and whose misdeeds often escaped with miserably insufficient punishment. Their authority, however, was not confined to ecclesiastical persons, numerous as these were. It extended to the laity also in all spiritual and moral offences and in certain civil cases (such as those relating to marriage and wills) which affected everyday life. Whatever might have been said for this jurisdiction in an earlier and ruder age, it was now to a large extent an anachronism. The royal administration had become strong enough to afford protection to all,

The ecclesiastical courts.

while the ecclesiastical tribunals were degenerate and corrupt, and were accused of gross partiality and still grosser extortion.

Such a condition of things could not last. The contrast between clerical privileges and clerical failings was too glaring. Moreover, the church was still mediæval at a time when things mediæval were passing away. The movement for reform, stifled by the French and Civil wars, was bound to recur when peace and quiet were restored.

In the latter part of the fifteenth century the impulse of the Renaissance, and in particular of that factor in it known as the Revival of Letters or Revival of Learning, began to be felt in England. By that Revival a vast intellectual awakening was implied. The ancient classics were made the object of study, Greek, which had been practically an unknown language in the middle ages, being raised to the chief place of honour, while the "Schoolmen" or mediæval theologians were scorned as barbarous and rude. It was at Oxford that the "new studies" found a centre. The credit of establishing them there belongs largely to William Grocyn, who had come under their influence when in Italy. Amongst others who were associated with him in his work was Thomas Linacre, who was a man of extraordinary powers, being alike "Latinist and Grecian, grammarian and physician". Linacre afterwards became the founder of the College of Physicians. The "New Learning" had important consequences. By it the intellect was quickened and made more conscious than it had been before of the superstition and ecclesiastical corruptions that prevailed. It was also seen how widely the church of the day had diverged in dogma as well as practice from that of the early ages.

In Oxford in 1497–98 there was resident a small body of earnest men, who realized the need of a speedy and radical change. Chief among these "Oxford Reformers" were John Colet, Erasmus, and Thomas More, who was still almost a youth. Colet was the fervent preacher, insisting on Christianity as the rule and guide of life. To him the Bible was a living book, not a mere collection of isolated texts. His soul abhorred the mediæval theologians with their barren speculations, their endless quibbles about words and phrases, their hair-splitting subtleties. "Keep to the Bible and the Apostles' Creed," was his practical advice, "and let divines, if they like, dispute about the rest." It was his desire that the clergy themselves should set the example in the way of reform. In 1505 he was appointed Dean of St. Paul's, London. Seeing the defects of the old system of education, he devoted his fortune to endowing a school in St. Paul's Churchyard, in which boys should be treated with kindness, and trained in Christian habits and good sound literature. His foundation, which served as a model for later institutions, was a secular one; his friend Lilly was its first headmaster.

The Oxford Reformers.

Erasmus was the scholar and theologian. By birth he was a native of Rotterdam, but it was from the English Colet that his mind received the bent which afterwards characterized it. Conscious of the faults and errors of the Latin Vulgate, which was then the only version of the Scriptures, Erasmus set himself to provide a more accurate text. His New Testament, which first appeared in 1516, was the result of his toil. It comprised, in addition to the Greek text, a new translation in Latin, and numerous paraphrases, notes, and comments. The work was one of vast importance. Inspired by the scholarship and learning of the Renaissance, it impeached the authority of the Vulgate, which had hitherto been regarded as infallible, and which, with its misconceptions and mistranslations, lay at the basis of the existing system. It rapidly went through several editions, and greatly promoted and strengthened the cause of reform.

More was the political philosopher of the Oxford band. His *Utopia*, which was written in 1515–16, and which in outward form is a description of the ideal state of Utopia ("Nowhere"), may be regarded as embodying their views on political and social problems. In it More has, in his own peculiar fashion, inextricably mingled jest and seriousness together. Wild, impracticable schemes of communism are found side by side with more sober measures and with arrangements which foreshadow the reforms of much later ages. In the Utopian commonwealth, although no idleness is allowed, men are not beasts of burden, but have their hours of labour limited to nine a day; disease is reduced to a minimum by good sanitary arrangements; the houses are bright and airy, and the streets "twenty foot broad"; judicial penalties are not cruel and barbarous, but vary in proportion to the offence and aim at preventing its repetition; the education of the people is attended to. In religious matters a wide toleration prevails. Every citizen must believe in the existence of God and in the immortality of the soul, but beyond that opinion is left absolutely free, and the public services are of such a kind as to hurt no man's conscience. In all respects Utopia was a marked contrast to the England of More's day. *(More's Utopia.)*

Colet and his friends looked with hope to the accession of Henry VIII., who was known to be well inclined to the "New Learning". But that monarch, instead of reforming the church, was soon immersed in continental politics. In 1513, however, he took a much-needed step by depriving clerical murderers and housebreakers of their "benefit of clergy", thus bringing them under the ordinary law. Convocation resented the change, and at once attacked Standish, a friar, who spoke in its defence. Thereupon Henry himself interfered in the friar's behalf, and on a suggestion being made to refer the whole matter to the pope for settlement, he angrily rejected it, exclaiming, "We are by the sufferance of God King of England, and the kings of England in times past never had any superior but God". The incident was important as indicating the near end of the papal, and assertion of the royal supremacy.

Although the Oxford Reformers failed in their aims, the ecclesiastical problem did not sleep. Wolsey was far too clear-sighted not to perceive that reform was inevitable, and, with his conservative temper, he preferred that it should come from within the church rather than be imposed on it in a more violent form from without. It was partly with a view of giving effect to this policy that he obtained the authority of cardinal and papal legate, and strove to get the papacy itself. The steps which he actually took were significant. He saw that the days of monasticism, as it then existed, were numbered, and that its wealth might with advantage be diverted to other objects.

Wolsey's proposed reforms. The process had already begun. William of Wykeham had dissolved certain religious houses to build New College, Oxford, and Winchester College. The alien priories had been confiscated by Henry V. and their revenues employed by his son in founding King's College, Cambridge, and Eton College. Wolsey carried out a still more sweeping conversion of monastic property. All religious houses which contained seven inmates or less he suppressed, as being no longer of service to the nation, and with the funds thus acquired he proposed to establish two colleges, one at Ipswich his birth-place, and the other at Oxford. It was also his purpose to remodel the system of teaching at the two universities. His fall, however, came before his plans had been realized. In spite of his entreaties the money he had collected was seized under the præmunire for the royal exchequer; his college at Ipswich was never built, and Cardinal College, his foundation at Oxford, only survived on a diminished scale under the name of Christ Church, with Henry, instead of himself, as founder. His attempt to deal with the abuses of the ecclesiastical courts by means of his legatine power was even more unfortunate. His authority was contested by Warham, Archbishop of Canterbury, and nothing but confusion was the result.

On the Continent, meanwhile, the long-expected explosion had taken place. In 1517 Martin Luther issued his protest against the monstrous sale of indulgences.[1] Rome answered his cry for reform by excommunicating

---

[1] Indulgences were papal letters granting remission of the penances due for sins: to compound toilsome penances for money was of course a gross abuse.

him, and by calling on the emperor Charles V. to crush him by force. In a short time a large part of Germany was in revolt against the papal see. The religious strife spread and deepened. In 1521 Henry VIII., who prided himself on his theological learning, threw himself into the contest by writing a treatise against Luther in defence of the Seven Sacraments, and received in consequence from Pope Leo X. the title of "Defender of the Faith". But however favourable he might be to the current doctrine of the church, he was fully alive to the mischief springing from the overgrown wealth and power of the clergy, which he regarded with jealousy and dislike. Moreover, the influence of the Lutheran movement began to be felt in England as in other countries. At Cambridge there arose a band of "gospellers",—men distinguished for their zeal in preaching, and warm supporters of the "new" opinions. Among them were Barnes, Latimer, and Coverdale, all of whom became famous as reformers. In 1526 an English version of the New Testament appeared. It was the work of William Tyndale, who thus enabled his countrymen to read the Scriptures for themselves. Reforming views, though condemned as "heresy", steadily gained ground. *[margin: The German Reformation.]*

In November 1529, immediately after the disgrace of Wolsey, who had depressed the national assembly, a new parliament met, which by its achievements has earned for itself the name of the Reformation Parliament. It lasted with prorogations for the unprecedented period of six and a half years, and in importance it is equalled, if at all, only by the Long Parliament of Charles I. The first session opened with the intimation by Sir Thomas More, who had succeeded the Cardinal as chancellor, that Henry would carry out an ecclesiastical reform. As the question had, in spite of the warnings of Gascoigne and Colet, been neglected by the clergy, it was now taken up by the king and Parliament. A beginning was made by forbidding spiritual persons to farm or trade for lucre's sake, by curtailing the "outrageous" charges made by them for *[margin: The Reformation Parliament.]*

probate of wills, and by prohibiting pluralities and non-residence, whereby, it was said, "one priest being little learned would have ten or twelve benefices and reside on none".

In the meantime Henry's suit for nullity of marriage remained undecided, and with it the course of the English Reformation became intermixed. Proceedings were still dragging on at the Roman court, whither the case had been revoked from before Wolsey and Campeggio. Catharine's nephew, the emperor, was urgent that the English king should be excommunicated. So far Henry had merely questioned the validity of the dispensation authorizing his marriage; he now went further, and denied the capacity of the pope to issue such a dispensation at all. Union with a brother's widow, being contrary to God's law, could not, he maintained, be made lawful by papal decree; consequently his marriage with Catharine was void from the outset. This new point was, apparently at the suggestion of Thomas Cranmer, a Cambridge lecturer in divinity, submitted to the universities of Europe for decision. Their replies, however, varied, the French theologians deciding in Henry's favour, the German against him (1530).

Continuance of the divorce question.

The reform measures of 1529 had been distasteful to the ecclesiastics; Fisher, Bishop of Rochester, openly hinted that they were due "to lack of faith only". In December of the next year a second and more important step was taken. The whole body of clergy were formally accused by the Crown of having violated the Statute of Præmunire by recognizing and submitting to the legateship of Wolsey. Quite taken aback by the charge, they were glad to buy their pardon by paying Henry a fine of nearly £119,000, and acknowledging him as *Supreme Head of the Church as far as the law of Christ allows*—"supremum caput quantum per Christi legem licet" (1531). The Commons were startled at the elastic character of the Præmunire, and procured an indemnity for themselves.

Henry "Supreme Head".

Henry was resolved to be undisputed master within his

realm. His difficulties seemed to thicken. Many of the clergy (especially among the "regulars"), besides being opposed to reform, preached openly in support of the pope's dispensing power. Catharine herself obstinately refused to give way or enter a convent. There was much feeling in her favour amongst the English, who saw their Flemish trade ruined through the hostility of her kinsman, Charles, and who, moreover, hated the new political connection which had been formed with France. "The common people daily murmured and spake their foolish fantasies." At the same time the tide of the Reformation continued to rise. Through all these years the printing-press was incessantly active. Tyndale's Testament, and the writings of Wyclif, Huss, Luther, and other reformers, were published in great quantities and circulated on all sides. Efforts to stamp them out only proved futile.

After a year's interval the attack on the privileged position of the clergy began afresh. The Commons, perhaps at Henry's instigation, presented a "*Supplication against the Ordinaries*", setting forth the wrongs and grievances of the lay estate in connection with the judicial and legislative powers of the spiritualty (1532). Convocation at first ventured on a reply, but ultimately made a full *Submission* to the king, undertaking not to enact canons in the future without his assent, and agreeing to the revision of those already in existence. Its legislation was henceforward to be under royal control. In principle, the Submission was no innovation, but was a revival of one of the rules or "precepts" by which William the Conqueror had essayed to curb the church's power. *The submission of the clergy.*

While the clergy thus lost their legislative independence, Parliament cut away further portions of their obnoxious judicial privileges. The practice of citing persons outside their own diocese was checked; and a wholesome restriction of benefit of clergy was effected by withdrawing it from all who were under the rank of subdeacon. The same session also saw the first enactment directly levelled at the papal connection. On the petition of the clergy a bill was passed abolishing the *annates*, or first-fruits, paid by each new archbishop and bishop to the Roman curia. This impost, which had been systematized by the papacy in the fourteenth century, amounted in each case to the first year's income of the see. The Annates Bill was merely provisional, Henry being empowered to enforce it or not as he chose. It was an instrument for exerting pressure on the prevaricating Pope Clement.

These measures were regarded with increasing dislike by partisans of the old regime. More, in disapproval of them, gave up the Great Seal, which he had held since Wolsey's dismissal. Being of a quiet turn of mind, the spread of reforming views, sometimes violent in character, had frightened him into conservatism. While in office he had disregarded the tolerant principles he had laid down in the Utopia, and had persecuted Lutherans and "heretics". His retirement left Thomas Cromwell incontestably the first in influence about the king. The son of a blacksmith and fuller of Putney, Cromwell was, like Wolsey, a man of the middle class. His life had been a chequered one. He had served as a soldier in Italy, and as a clerk at Antwerp; then for a time he had carried on the trade of a fuller; he had lent money; afterwards he had become a lawyer. By his capacity he attracted the notice of Wolsey, who employed him as his principal agent in dissolving the small monasteries. When his patron fell, Cromwell defended him in Parliament, and thereby won Henry's regard and was admitted to his service. He was a practical, hard-headed man, shrewd, acute, and with great ability for business. He soon rose to be royal secretary, "bearing most rule of all other under the king".

Rise of Thomas Cromwell.

Meanwhile Henry's relations with the papacy grew more and more strained. He had already ceased to live with Catharine as queen. In November 1532, Clement, yielding to her entreaties, issued a brief commanding him to take her back under pain of excommunication. The menace was disregarded by the English king, who had just met Francis in an interview at Calais, and was assured of the French alliance. Warham having lately died, Henry nominated Cranmer as his successor at Canterbury, and by threatening to put the Annates Bill in force compelled Clement to confirm the appointment. He had waited six years for the settlement of his marriage-suit, and his patience was at last worn out. The pope's double-dealing irritated him. In March 1533 an Act of Parliament was passed, which, after reciting the evils of appeals to Rome, "the great delay and let to the true and speedy determination of the causes", prohibited appeals in cases relating to wills, matrimony, or oblations. Such cases were to be settled within the country itself. It was not long before the new archbishop was commissioned to try "the king's matter". In May 1533 he held his court at Dunstable, and gave judgment that the marriage with Catharine was invalid and void from the first, and that Henry was lawfully united to Anne Boleyn. The king had secretly wedded Anne some months before. Cranmer declares Henry divorced.

The breach with Rome widened. Henry paid no heed when Clement signed the sentence of excommunication against him which the emperor had demanded, but pressed steadily on in his course. The papal supremacy, having shown itself antagonistic to national interests and to ecclesiastical reform, was irrevocably doomed. In the following spring (1534) came an important series of statutes which in effect abolished it. (1) The Act for the Submission of the Clergy gave the authority of law to the Submission which Convocation had made to Henry two years before. It repeated the provision for revising the canons, and declared such of them to be abrogated as were "contrariant to the king's prerogative" or to the customs and statutes of the realm. This enactment threw the canon law into utter confusion, no one knowing what had been annulled by it and what not. Another clause of the same Act extended the former partial Statute of Appeals, by forbidding *all* appeals Anti-papal legislation.

to Rome "of what nature, condition, or quality soever". Ecclesiastical causes were to be determined in the last resort by royal commissioners sitting in Chancery. (2) A second Act made the Annates Bill absolute, the annates themselves being shortly afterwards transferred to the king. It also prescribed a fresh mode of electing and consecrating prelates. Hitherto elections, though nominally free, had in reality been controlled by the king or the pope. All interference on the part of the latter was now stopped. On a see falling vacant, the sovereign was empowered to send a *congé d'élire* (or license to make a new election) to the chapter, and with it a letter missive naming the person whom they must elect or run the risk of a præmunire. The chapter's part in the election was thus merely formal, the real power resting with the king. (3) A third statute swept away papal licenses, and all "pensions, Peter-pence, or any other impositions" paid to the "Bishop of Rome". It effectually put an end to the drain of English money into papal coffers.

In the same session Parliament also confirmed Henry's marriage with Anne, and passed an Act of Succession entailing the crown on their joint issue. About the same time the pope at length delivered judgment as to Julius' dispensation, pronouncing it to be valid and the king's first marriage consequently good. He had taken seven years to decide the point.

The radical changes of the last five years could not fail to cause discontent within the realm. Sympathy with Catharine, Spanish intrigues, clerical dissatisfaction at loss of privileges, papal influence, all tended to the same result. In the background, too, dynastic hostility to the Tudors was always present. Families of Plantagenet descent were continually on the watch for an opportunity to grasp at the crown. The various elements of opposition needed only to be brought into one centre, or supported by foreign help, to become a serious danger to the king. Of all the malcontents no one denounced Henry with greater violence than Elizabeth Barton, the "Nun of Kent". Formerly a servant at Aldington, near

Canterbury, the Nun had become the tool of a knot of intriguing monks and friars. Being subject to epileptic fits, she was given out to be inspired and a saint, and her prophecies against the king were circulated throughout the land. For three years she was not interfered with, and then she and her chief accomplices were arrested and destroyed by an Act of Attainder (1534). Her utterances were dangerous from their probable effect on the masses, who were, as Chapuys, the emperor's ambassador, declared, "peculiarly credulous and easily moved to insurrections by prophecies". *The "Nun of Kent".*

All peril was not yet over. Rome was too powerful to submit quietly to the curtailment of her empire. A bull deposing Henry and releasing his subjects from their allegiance was being prepared. Charles was strongly urged to invade England; and in order to prevent this, a French fleet during the summer (1534) kept watch in the Channel. In Ireland a fierce rebellion had broken out under the leadership of Lord Thomas Fitzgerald. With affairs in this state it was all the more necessary to guard against papal and imperial intrigues at home. A stringent oath, based on the Act of Succession, was drawn up and tendered to all whose loyalty was suspected. In November Parliament reassembled for a brief session, in which it rounded off its former work by the Act of Supremacy.

Nearly four years before the clergy, when threatened with the præmunire, had acknowledged Henry as Supreme Head, but with the important limitation *as far as the law of Christ allows*. That limitation now disappeared. The Act of Supremacy declared that the king "was the only Supreme Head in earth of the Church of England", and should enjoy the title thereof and all "pre-eminences, jurisdictions, and commodities" belonging thereto. Besides attributing to him this extensive authority, it also invested him with power to "visit, correct, and reform" ecclesiastical "errors, abuses, and enormities". To offend against the statute was treason.

The breach with Rome was now complete. It had long been foreshadowed: Henry's marriage-question had been the occasion, not the cause, of it. The papal supremacy, which had by a series of usurpations imposed itself upon England, had now been entirely thrown off. Its continuance was obnoxious to patriotic feeling and incompatible with true national autonomy. Henceforth England was to be independent ecclesiastically as well as politically. English bishoprics and livings were not, as in the past, to be possessed by foreigners and papal nominees, who rarely, if ever, set foot in the country. At the same time the corrupt condition of the clergy had been dealt with. Their *imperium in imperio* was now at an end. They had been brought under the ordinary law and subjected to the king, who, as head of the nation, had also become the head of the church. The royal had replaced the papal supremacy.

The breach with Rome.

The ease with which such mighty changes had been effected proves that Henry had the bulk of the nation on his side. Against such discontent as existed he acted with promptness. An oath of supremacy, acknowledging his title as head of the church, was made the test of loyalty. As the religious orders had always been the firmest supporters of papal claims, it was presented to them first of all. For refusing to take it the priors of three Carthusian monasteries were at once sent to the block. After an interval two far more distinguished persons, Fisher, Bishop of Rochester, and the learned Sir Thomas More, declining to accept the oath, suffered the same fate. The bishop's attitude had been rugged and uncompromising throughout. A staunch champion of Catharine and the papal cause, he had held intercourse with the Nun of Kent, and been in suspicious correspondence with the envoy of Henry's enemy, the emperor. His last act was to accept a cardinal's hat from the pope in defiance of England's abjuration of him. More's opposition had been of a far quieter kind. Objecting to the reformation in the shape which it assumed, he had receded from his former liberal views, and died in defence of a condition of things which he himself had denounced (1535).

Execution of More and Fisher.

Henry, true to the policy of his house, had struck at the leading figures among the malcontents. The effect was immediate. Whatever resistance might have been met with quickly disappeared. In vain did "Christ's Vicegerent", Paul III., rave and call for help to deprive the "heretic" of his kingdom. Francis had too formidable an enemy in Charles to sacrifice his alliance with the English; and the emperor himself was fully occupied with his war against the Turkish sultan. Moreover Henry, as a counterpoise to any league the pope might draw together against him, opened negotiations for an alliance with the reformed states of Germany. The latter were already known by the name of Protestant.

Catharine, who had for years been sickly, did not long survive her deposition. In January 1536 she died, and thus a constant source of trouble for Henry was removed. Meanwhile the king's hopes of a son had been disappointed, the only issue of his second marriage being a daughter, Elizabeth. His love for Anne rapidly cooled, especially as she displayed an arrogance which he could not tolerate. Intrigue was also busy at work to overthrow her. In May 1536 she was arrested, and condemned to death on charges of flagrant immorality, which derived their weight from the free manners of the age. On the day following her execution Henry was betrothed to Jane Seymour, a Wiltshire lady "of sweet disposition", but "of no great beauty, and not even tolerably pretty".

Fall of Anne Boleyn.

CHAPTER IV.

THE DICTATORSHIP (1535-47).

Since the close of 1533 Thomas Cromwell had been the chief minister of the king. Already the foremost man in the realm politically, he became so in ecclesiastical matters also, when in 1535 Henry as Supreme

Head appointed him his "Vicegerent, Vicar-General, and principal Commissary in causes ecclesiastical". It was his task as Vicar-General to carry out the Act of Supremacy and the policy involved in it.

Cromwell addressed himself to his fresh duties with characteristic energy. He proceeded to enforce obedience on the clergy, who naturally resented the loss of their privileges, and, to guard against their fomenting discontent, he issued orders regulating their freedom of preaching, and directing them "to set forth God's Word" and the new title of the king. This plan of controlling or "tuning" the pulpits was adopted in view of the enormous influence which was then exercised by them, and which was often used, as in the days of De Montfort and Thomas of Lancaster, for merely political purposes. Further, in 1536 Cromwell sent out injunctions to the clergy, directing them to teach the Creed, the Lord's Prayer, and the Ten Commandments in the English tongue, and to provide an English Bible for their churches. The translation of the Scriptures referred to was probably that by Coverdale, a friend of Tyndale. Hitherto Bibles in English had been forbidden books.

The English Bible.

So far the English Reformation, unlike the continental, had been political and legal in character: it had not touched doctrine. In 1536 the process of purifying the tenets of the church began. In that year the Ten Articles were published, which declared the Bible and the three Creeds to be the sole authority in matters of faith, and specified three sacraments only as generally necessary to salvation, viz. baptism, penance, and the sacrament of the altar. The Ten Articles showed the influence of the "New Learning". They left much room for honest differences of opinion, and were in marked contrast with the dogmas of the middle ages.

Meanwhile the religious question had given birth to much controversy. Gardiner, who had been Wolsey's secretary and was now Bishop of Winchester, strongly defended the royal supremacy in his *De Vera Obedientia*

(1535). He rejected the claims of the " Bishop of Rome" as false, and argued on the triple ground of reason, of history, and of Holy Scripture, that the temporal prince, as head of the realm, must be head of the church also. The chief advocate on the opposite side was Reginald Pole in his book on Unity, *Pro Ecclesiasticae Unitatis Defensione*. Pole was, as far as doctrine was concerned, a reformer, and had only espoused the papal cause after some hesitation. He was of Yorkist descent, his mother being the daughter of George of Clarence, the brother of Edward IV.

On other points the strife of opinion grew keen. The publication of the Scriptures in English, by showing Christianity in its pure and original form, increased rather than lessened it. Transubstantiation, the mediæval dogma as to the Eucharist, was inevitably attacked, as it had already been by Wyclif and Luther. It was materialistic in colour, and asserted that in the Sacrament a change of substance is effected, the bread becoming the actual body, and the wine the actual blood, of Christ. To this tenet Henry firmly adhered, sending the learned Frith and others who rejected it to the stake. He thus steered a kind of middle course between two extremes. On the one hand he beheaded those who opposed his Supremacy as traitors, and on the other he burnt deniers of transubstantiation as heretics. This attitude he maintained till his death.

In England monasticism had long been showing unmistakable signs of corruption and decay. For more than a century it had not produced a single person of eminence. Many suppressions had already for various reasons taken place; so that by 1535 only about seven hundred houses out of a total of twelve hundred still continued to exist, and of these many were mismanaged and were sinking more and more hopelessly into debt. The number of monastic inmates had declined, in spite of efforts—including even the kidnapping of children—to keep it up. The monks, too, no longer led the way, as they had done in former ages, in

The English Monasteries.

spiritual matters, in education, and in economics, but were rather an obstacle to religious and social progress. Their general character, as Wyclif, Gascoigne, and the Oxford Reformers alike testify, was one of laziness, ignorance, self-indulgence, and bigotry. The religious houses were often disturbed by squabbles and factions; the monastic rules were badly kept; discipline was lax. Some of the houses, as perhaps was inevitable among a large celibate body, were disgraced by immorality and vice. Archbishop Morton had found a scandalous state of things prevailing in the great abbey of St. Alban's; and shortly before 1535 traces of moral laxity were revealed in the abbeys of Dorchester, Thame, and Leicester.

No part of the church stood more in need of reform than the monasteries. They owned extensive estates and had usurped much, perhaps nearly one-half, of the tithes which should have supported the parochial clergy. Their wealth was great, and with that wealth, if they did no harm, they did little or no good.

Directly after his appointment as Vicar-General, Cromwell had nominated a body of commissioners to visit and inquire into the state of the monasteries. The task was Abolition of the Lesser Houses. quickly carried out; and a report was drawn up and laid before Parliament, depicting in black colours the condition of the lesser houses. Thereupon that assembly, "considering the manifest sin and vicious living committed in the small monasteries" and the "little or no amendment" hitherto effected, passed an Act by which such of them as had not a yearly income of more than £200 were suppressed and their possessions given to the king for other uses.

This statute was the last great measure of the Reformation Parliament, which, after lasting since November 1529, now came to an end. To deal with the property which had thus been transferred to the Crown, a special court, the Court of Augmentations, was created. But the work of dissolving the monasteries had not proceeded far, when it was interrupted by the outbreak of rebellion.

The scene of the insurrection lay in the north, which

was then the least advanced part of England. It was there that the power of the clergy and gentry was greatest. Several causes—religious, political, and social—had combined to bring about the outbreak. Each class of the community had grievances of its own. The clergy were discontented at the curtailment of their wealth and privileges which had taken place. The nobles were angry at being eclipsed in authority and influence by Cromwell, whom they detested as a man of "base blood" and longed to overthrow. The great land-owners were aggrieved by the recent Statute of Uses, which restricted their power of settling or disposing of their estates or of leaving them by will. The lower orders were suffering from an agrarian crisis, resulting from the break-up of the mediæval land-system and the conversion of arable land into pasture. But the most prominent cause of all, and that which gave to the movement the name of the *Pilgrimage of Grace*, was the religious one. The monasteries were not unpopular in the north, and their forcible suppression produced grave discontent. All sorts of wild rumours, "slanderous tales, and feigned fables", were industriously circulated to fan the flame.

The Pilgrimage of Grace.

The insurrection first began in Lincolnshire at the end of September 1536, but there it collapsed almost at once. It immediately broke out in a far more formidable shape in Yorkshire and the north, where it received the name of the Pilgrimage of Grace, from the cognizance or badge of the five wounds of Christ assumed by the rebels. Its leader was Robert Aske, a barrister, who seems to have acted out of genuine feeling for the masses. For a time there was no resistance. To the number of thirty thousand the insurgents advanced to seize Doncaster and the line of the Don, which commanded the entrance into Yorkshire from the midlands. Here, however, they found their progress barred by the swollen waters of the river, and by a royal army with artillery under the command of the Duke of Norfolk. Negotiations ensued, the "pilgrims" complaining of the suppression of so many religious houses, of the Statute of Uses, and of the introduction into the Council of Cromwell and other "personages of low birth and small reputation". Jealousies soon showed themselves between the gentry and the commonalty; and upon Henry promising a general pardon and a fresh parliament, the rebels dispersed under the impression that they had gained most of their demands. They were quickly undeceived. The cry was raised that "they had been betrayed by the gentlemen", and several spasmodic risings followed. These were easily crushed. The general pardon was recalled; martial law was put in force; and Aske and others were executed. Strong measures were taken to reduce and hold down the troublesome north. To curb the nobles a new tribunal, the Council of the North, was created. This court in later years did an important work in breaking down the remnants of feudalism, and securing the undisputed supremacy of law and order in the district beyond the Humber.

<small>Suppression of the Rising.</small>

For a time the revolt had seemed likely to be supported by foreign help. On hearing of it the pope had despatched Pole, who was now a cardinal, to urge Francis and the regent of the Netherlands to attack England. James V., the king of Scotland, actually held some communications with the disaffected gentry of the north, and boasted that he "would within a year break spears" with Henry, his uncle. The movement, however, was crushed before any external assistance could arrive.

The rising had little effect on the course pursued by the king and his minister. The Statute of Uses was not repealed, although in 1540 it was modified. The dissolution of the religious fraternities whose annual income did not exceed £200, was pushed rapidly forward. On the greater houses a stricter discipline was enforced. So irksome did this prove to them, that they began to surrender themselves one by one into the king's hands. In some cases at least their action was hastened by pressure or coercion. These proceedings were confirmed in 1539 by an Act vesting in Henry all the monastic foundations which had already been, or which should afterwards be, dissolved or surrendered. Before long there was not a single monastery left.

The monastic suppression had been on national grounds justifiable and necessary; still it was, in the mode in which it was carried out, marked by much harshness and greed. The royal agents, of whom Layton, Legh, London, and Ap Rice were the chief, often acted overbearingly and coarsely. There was much embezzlement, and prices, owing to the numerous sales, were low, so that Henry did not receive nearly the full value of the property transferred to him. The money which was actually paid into his Court of Augmentations was expended on various objects. More than half of it went in war expenses, in constructing fortifications for the defence of the coasts, in making guns, and in supplying a great national want by the creation of a fleet. Large sums also were spent on the royal household. Some small amounts were used for religious or educational purposes. Six new bishoprics were set up;[1] some endowments were bestowed on the Universities of Oxford and Cambridge; and several grammar-schools were founded for the education of the young. *The Monastic Property.*

The results of the suppression were important. It decided the quarrel between the secular and regular clergy, which had lasted since the time of Dunstan, in favour of the seculars. It destroyed the ecclesiastics' command of the House of Lords, the majority in which now shifted, upon the disappearance of the parliamentary abbots, from the spiritual to the lay peers. It also marked an era in social and agrarian history. On the spoils of the monasteries a new nobility arose, which was bound by self-interest to uphold Henry's work. The land, which had been locked up in the possession of monastic corporations, passed to individual owners, and became to a far greater extent than before an article of commerce. The new landlords were less easy-going than the monks had been. They farmed *Results of the Dissolution.*

---

[1] Oxford, Peterborough, Chester, Gloucester, Bristol, and the ephemeral see of Westminster.

or managed their estates with a view to profit, adopting the new or improved methods denoted by the general name of "inclosures". The Dukes of Suffolk and Norfolk, the Earl of Rutland, the Seymours and the Dudleys were among the largest acquirers of monastic property.

In other respects, too, the process of purifying and reforming the church continued. Great numbers of relics were destroyed, by which the clergy—especially the monks—had imposed on the credulity of the populace. Shrines were demolished, and the privilege of sanctuary, which enabled criminals to escape from justice, was reduced to very narrow limits.

At last, in October 1537, a son Edward was born to Henry, although at the cost of the life of the queen, Jane Seymour. The birth of an heir-apparent was a sore disappointment to those families which had claims on the succession. Signs of restlessness appeared among the Courtenays, the Nevills, and the Poles, who were all of Yorkist blood and closely connected together. On the Continent the pope had just made peace between Francis and Charles, and was endeavouring to unite those monarchs in a war against Henry. An intrigue was opened between the English malcontents and Cardinal Pole, the pope's agent, but before any action could be taken it was detected, and Henry Courtenay, Marquis of Exeter, and Henry Pole, Lord Montague, were arrested and executed. The danger of a foreign attack still remained. James of Scotland took up a threatening attitude, while in Flanders ships and munitions of war were busily collected for an invasion of England.

Affairs were in this state when Parliament met (April 1539) and passed the Act of Proclamations and the Act of the Six Articles, besides transferring to Henry the greater monasteries which surrendered. The king had always enjoyed a certain power of issuing regulations to supplement the law. By the Act of Proclamations an extension of this power was sanctioned. Proclamations, issued with the assent of the Privy Council, and not prejudicing the lives or possessions of

The Six Articles.

subjects or infringing any law or custom, were to have the force of statutes. Henry had already received from Parliament the privilege of appointing his successor by will: now he was able, within certain definite limits, to legislate. The Tudor monarchy had reached its culminating point.

The Six Articles, or, as they were termed by reformers, "the Whip with Six Strings", professedly aimed at quieting the religious controversy which was raging in the country. They were a sequel to the Ten Articles, but were far more narrow and dogmatic in tone. They determined, in accordance with mediæval teaching, several points which had been left free and open to the individual conscience in the prior measure. (1) The theory of transubstantiation was affirmed; (2) communion in both kinds was declared not to be essential to salvation; (3) priests were not to have wives; (4) vows of chastity were irrevocable; (5) private masses and (6) auricular confession were expedient and necessary. Severe penalties were fixed for offences against the Articles, a denial of transubstantiation being punishable by death.

The alliance between France and Spain had caused Henry to draw towards the German Protestants. It was Cromwell's plan to meet the threatening papal combination by forming a league of reformed states, with England at its head. With a view to this object he brought about a marriage between his master and Anne, sister of the Duke of Cleves—a ruler who had great influence in the Protestant world, and whose dominions commanded the course of the Rhine and shut off Charles' Hapsburg territories from his possessions in Flanders. *Henry's fourth marriage.* The step proved an unfortunate one. No political results such as Cromwell had hoped for followed from it. The king was shocked by Anne's ugliness and want of breeding. He had never really liked the German connection, and upon a fresh quarrel occurring between Francis and the emperor, that connection lost all value for him.

For some time Cromwell's influence with Henry had

been on the wane. He was an ardent reformer, and wished for further religious changes, to which the king was opposed. The Six Articles had been a distinct rebuff to him. After the failure of his diplomacy he lost Henry's favour, and was abandoned, as Wolsey had been, to his enemies, who were numerous and powerful. By the old nobility and by "certain of the clergy he was detestably hated". In July 1540 he was beheaded as a traitor and heretic. Only three months before he had been created Earl of Essex. About the same time Henry freed himself from Anne by means of a divorce.[1]

<small>Fall of Cromwell.</small>

Cromwell was essentially a home minister — not a diplomatist. In the main events of the Reformation, the separation from Rome, and the vindication and enforcement of the royal Supremacy, he had taken the leading part. He had also carried out the dissolution of the monasteries that remained. His methods were brusque and despotic. Throughout "the Hammer of the Monks" had laboured faithfully and consistently to make his master absolute in church as well as state.

As minister Cromwell had no successor, his place being in a sense taken by the Council as a whole. The two most prominent councillors were Norfolk and Gardiner, both of whom were adverse to doctrinal reform. For the rest of the reign the Six Articles remained on the statute-book, but they were enforced only spasmodically. Apparently about thirty persons suffered death under the "Bloody Statute", and all of them seem to have been deniers of transubstantiation. Among the number was Anne Askew, a well-born and highly-educated lady. She refused to abjure her "heresy", and was burnt declaring "I am persuaded it (*i.e.* the bread) cannot be God".

The French alliance formed by Wolsey had been of great service to Henry in his quarrel with the emperor

---

[1] Henry then married a niece of the Duke of Norfolk, Catharine Howard, who was shortly afterwards condemned and beheaded for unchastity. After her death he took his sixth and last wife, Catharine Parr, the Dowager Lady Latimer. She was a young widow of blameless manners and great tact, and was the uneasy partner of Henry's last five years.

and the pope. It had also ensured quiet on the side of Scotland. The king of that country, James V., was restless and ambitious. Making it his object to crush the power of his nobles, he was forced to rely more and more upon the clergy for support. **War with Scotland.**

His attitude to the reform measures of Henry was one of hostility. Gradually he was won over to the side of the pope. An English match was offered him, but through the influence of Archbishop Beaton and the clergy he rejected it, and in 1538 married Mary, daughter of the Duke of Guise, one of the bitterest enemies of the Reformation. Henceforward Scottish policy was, except at intervals, controlled by Beaton and the Guises.

An open breach with England soon came. James sent help to the Irish rebels, and began to negotiate for a continental alliance. In the hope of settling matters Henry arranged a personal interview with him at York, but James failed to appear (1541). The English king was deeply irritated. War with France was imminent, and he resolved to overpower the ally of France before it began. Reviving Edward I.'s claim to suzerainty over Scotland, he despatched Norfolk with 30,000 troops across the border (1542). It was a rash act, and the invaders were soon compelled by lack of supplies to retire. James was at once eager for a counter-raid into England, but his lords refused to follow him. The prelates, however, were more compliant, and by their efforts 10,000 men were gathered together and poured into Cumberland. The command was given to Oliver Sinclair, a royal favourite. Discontent and insubordination ensued, and the whole host fled away in panic before a few hundred Cumbrian farmers, the main body rushing into Solway Moss, and being either cut down or captured. This disgrace broke James's heart. As he lay dying he received the news of the birth of a daughter. "The deil take it," he muttered, referring to his crown, "it came with a lass and it will go with a lass!"

Henry did not make a harsh use of his victory. Falling back, as he had done after Flodden, on pacific methods, he proposed a marriage between his son Edward and Mary, the infant princess of Scotland. The captives taken at Solway Moss were released on the understanding that they would forward his project. For a time all went well. Beaton was imprisoned; Arran, the regent, professed loyal intentions to Henry; and in July 1543 a treaty of marriage was actually arranged.

Meanwhile hostilities had again blazed out between Charles and the French king, who was now leagued with the Turks. For some time Henry's relations with Francis **Henry's last war with France.** had been growing strained. That monarch refused to pay him his debts, and moreover was actively working against him in Scotland. Hence in 1543 Henry allied with the emperor against their common enemy.

This recurrence of war between England and France caused the Scottish hatred of the English to break out afresh. Beaton was set free; the fickle Arran, "some deal variant", trimmed to the French side; and in the end the marriage treaty just concluded was repudiated by the Scots. To punish them, Lord Hertford, brother of Jane Seymour, was sent northwards before the campaign on the Continent opened. Transporting his army by sea, he disembarked at Leith, sacked and burnt Edinburgh, and returned by land, "destroying every pile, fortress, and village in his walk". Such measures only increased the stubbornness of the Scots, and a pitiless warfare raged along the borders.

The chief scene of operations lay abroad. Rejecting plans which were drawn up merely in the emperor's interest, Henry laid siege to Boulogne, to provide a secure base of action for himself and at the same time increase his command of the narrow seas. The place no sooner fell into his hands than he found himself deserted by Charles, who made peace with France. He was now left to face his enemies single-handed. Boulogne was **Capture of Boulogne.** vigorously assaulted by the French. The Scots, encouraged by a trifling victory at Ancrum Muir (1545) and by the arrival of help from

France, prepared for an inroad into the northern counties. A French armament of 200 sail crossed the Channel, and forcing back the English fleet, effected a landing in the Isle of Wight. A papal congress, summoned to deal with the Reformation movement, was slowly assembling at Trent. In the presence of these dangers the spirit of the English nation rose. Boulogne was successfully held against all attempts to retake it. The French attack on the south coast was ruined by mismanagement and disease, while all fear of invasion from the north was removed by Hertford, who again crossed the border and ravaged the Lowlands of Scotland without resistance (Sept. 1545). Peace followed in June 1546, Francis agreeing to pay Henry an indemnity of 2,000,000 crowns within eight years, England meanwhile retaining Boulogne as security for the debt. Scotland was to be included in the pacification.

Henry, who was extravagant and free-handed in money matters, had been brought into grave financial straits by the war. In two years it had cost him £1,300,000. To meet the strain, besides mortgaging his estates, he adopted the course of debasing the coinage. Hitherto English money had been noted for its excellent quality: the disastrous effects of thus tampering with it were to unfold themselves in the following reigns. Moreover, in 1545, Parliament, to help him in his "inestimable charges and expenses", empowered him to take possession of the property of chantries and religious gilds. Henry, however, only availed himself to a small extent of the authority thus given him.

The principal foe of the English alliance in Scotland was Beaton, Archbishop of St. Andrews. He was also the chief opponent of the Reformation in that country, and brought great odium on himself by his persecutions. In May 1546 he was murdered in his castle of St. Andrews by a band of conspirators under Norman Leslie. His death, however, was to bring no advantage to Henry. The king was slowly dying, and was leaving the crown to his son Edward, a boy of nine years. The outlook proved too tempting for the loyalty of the Earl of Surrey and his father Norfolk, who entered into a plot to seize the government, if not the throne. Their scheming came to Henry's ears. Surrey was sent to the scaffold, and Norfolk was only saved from a similar fate by the decease of the king (January 1547).

During the last years of the reign, the liturgical reform, which had been begun by Cromwell's Injunctions of 1536, had been resumed. Cranmer had drawn up an English litany, and an English "primer" or book of private devotions had been published. Other changes in the same direction were in contemplation when Henry died.

Henry has been aptly described as "the king, the whole king, and nothing but the king". He was the English *grand monarque*. He had the vices of his age— **Henry's character.** cruelty, ingratitude, heartlessness. Men were to him little more than instruments. His was a strong rule; all parts of the administrative machine were made to move in obedience to his will. Yet he was no Nero: he had no standing army, like his contemporaries Francis and Charles. However arbitrary his acts might be, still he was the guardian of the national interests, and he never ceased to watch the current of popular feeling. He won or restored the ecclesiastical independence of his country. Under him Wales was finally incorporated in England, and Ireland raised to the rank of a kingdom. To the nobility, which had been so turbulent in the preceding century, he was severe and merciless. But commerce expanded, and the commons grew in wealth and importance under

> "the majestic lord
> That broke the bonds of Rome".

CHAPTER V.

THE MINORITY—EDWARD VI. (1547–1553).

England had now to taste the evils of a minority. By his will Henry had entailed the crown upon his three children, Edward, Mary, and Elizabeth, in succession, and then, passing over his elder sister Margaret of Scotland and her line, had bequeathed it to the descendants of his younger sister Mary, the late Duchess of Suffolk. As Edward was not yet ten years old, a Council of Regency was to govern until he came of age. *The will of Henry VIII.* The members of this Council, sixteen in number, Henry had carefully chosen from among men of different shades of religious opinion, in order to prevent any one section from becoming supreme. This arrangement was scarcely a practicable one in a country like England, which had grown accustomed to the centralisation of power in a single person. It was at once upset by Hertford, the young king's uncle, who persuaded his fellow councillors to appoint him Protector of the realm with almost unlimited authority. About the same time he created himself Duke of Somerset, and made his brother Thomas Lord Seymour of Sudleye and High Admiral.

The Protector's task was no easy one. He had four distinct difficulties to deal with, each of which demanded cautious statesmanship. These were the relations with Scotland and with France, the religious question and the social.

Before the late king's death negotiations had been again opened for the marriage of Edward and the young Scottish queen, Mary. The prospects of the match were not altogether hopeless; but to bring it about and so secure English predominance north of the Cheviots the exercise of unceasing vigilance and patience was necessary. For such a policy Somerset was eminently unfitted. Instead of firmly supporting the English party, he looked on without moving while French troops proceeded to Scotland, captured St. Andrews, which was being held by Norman Leslie as the ally of England, and established French influence in the country. The effects of his neglect he then proposed to undo by one heroic stroke—an invasion of Scotland. His ill-advised plan immediately united all

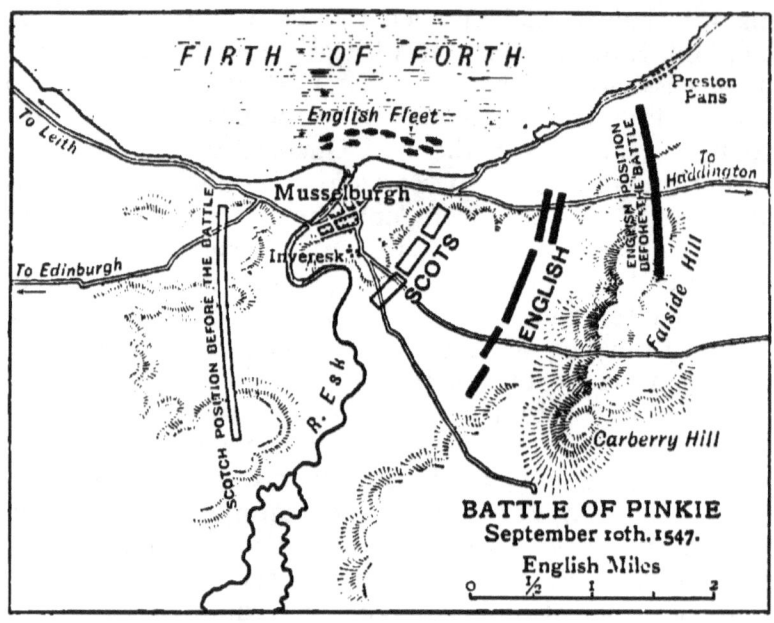

parties and all classes in opposition to him. "I dislike not the match," a Scotch noble is reported to have said, "but I hate the manner of wooing." Near Musselburgh Somerset found an army almost double his own in numbers drawn up to meet him behind the Esk. Advancing to seize the high ground about Inveresk he was thought by the Scots to be making for his fleet in Musselburgh Bay, and full of confidence they hurried across the stream to intercept him. He at once wheeled to the left, and securing the advantage of position attacked the enemy before they had time to re-form. Being crowded together, they soon

Battle of Pinkie.

broke and fled before the fire of the English artillery, arquebus-men, and archers. More than 10,000 of them perished. Such was the battle of Pinkie, the last and one of the bloodiest of the encounters between the English and Scotch before the union of the two crowns. Although Somerset had won a great victory he was defeated in his object. French reinforcements came to aid the Scots in continuing the struggle. Mary herself was sent to France, where in the course of the next year she was betrothed to the Dauphin, afterwards Francis II.

In dealing with the religious question the Protector showed himself scarcely less impetuous than in dealing with the Scottish. He was a reformer, and his elevation to the protectorate had marked the triumph of the reforming party in the Council over the conservative section, which desired to maintain ecclesiastical affairs exactly as Henry had left them. A series of rapid changes began. The Six Articles and other measures by which Henry had kept down the religious controversy were repealed. Even the Anti-Lollard legislation was swept away. An act was passed that prelates should in future be nominated directly by the Crown, instead of being chosen by the indirect method of *congé d'élire*. Steps were taken towards purifying the system of public worship, which was then mainly formal, consisting of outward shows, rites, and observances. Images were removed from the churches as tending to idolatry. Many gorgeous ceremonies were discontinued. The Latin mass was abolished and its place taken by a communion service in English. Chantries and gilds, which were connected with the saying of masses for the souls of the dead, were suppressed by Parliament on the ground of superstition, and their property given to the Crown for religious and educational purposes. Finally, in 1549, a Prayer Book entirely in English was published. By it ritual was greatly simplified. The old Latin services, which had been unintelligible to the people at large, were now altogether superseded.

Somerset and the Reformation.

These changes, however admirable in themselves, were accompanied by much plundering and destruction. Church property was seized or stolen by members of the Council and by officials of every grade. The Protector himself set the example by demolishing two churches in order to build Somerset House in the Strand. In vain did Latimer, the old Cambridge gospeller, inveigh against the peculation that prevailed, crying: "Make restitution; choose thou either restitution or else damnation". Gardiner, the ablest of the religious conservatives, was sent to the Tower. He had been purposely excluded from the Council of Regency by Henry, who distrusted him.

For some time an agrarian revolution had been passing over the face of the country. The modern competitive spirit was just arising, and under its influence the rigid agricultural system of the Middle Ages was breaking up. New methods of dealing with the soil were found to be more profitable than the old, and so were gradually adopted. The change was manifesting itself in three different forms, all of which were known by or included in the general name of "inclosures". These were: (1) **The Agrarian crisis.** the arrangement of arable ground in fenced closes, such as exist to-day, in the place of the strips in "open" or unenclosed fields; (2) the conversion of tilled land into pasture; and (3) the inclosing or appropriation by individual owners of *commons* or *wastes*, over which common rights existed. The throwing of arable into grazing land had begun in the preceding century. It was much stimulated after the year 1500 by the high price which wool then fetched in the market. Far more profit could be obtained by keeping sheep for the sake of their fleeces than by growing corn. Hence a process of amalgamating small holdings to form large grazing-farms set in. Tenants were evicted; labourers could no longer find work on the land; the population of rural villages decayed. "Your sheep," wrote Sir Thomas More in the *Utopia*, "that were wont to be so meek and tame, now eat up and swallow down the very men themselves. They consume, destroy, and devour whole fields, houses, and cities. . . . The husbandmen be thrust out of their own, or else either by covin and fraud or by violent oppression they be put beside it; . . . by one means or other they must needs depart away." Latimer, who was himself the son of a Leicestershire yeoman, speaks to a similar effect. "'These graziers, inclosers, rent-raisers, are hinderers of the king's honour, for where there have been a great many householders and inhabitants there is now but a shepherd and his dog. Such proceedings do intend plainly to make of the yeomanry slavery."

The substitution of pasturage for tillage was viewed with alarm. To check it numerous statutes had been passed, but, like the Licinian Rogations of ancient Rome, they were evaded or were of little effect. A single furrow would be driven across a broad plain to satisfy the requirement that it "must be under the plough". Economic forces were too strong for legislation to overcome. The change, although ultimately of benefit to the whole nation, yet at the time inflicted much distress upon the peasants. Not only did they lose their employment, but they were also robbed of rights which they possessed over the wastes, when these were fenced in by the lords. Many of them sank into vagrants. Their sufferings had been one of the elements in the Pilgrimage of Grace. After the death of Henry the great landowners were left without any control, and inclosures went on at a quickened rate. The ferment among the peasantry grew. Riots and disturbances ensued. The crisis, already a serious one, was aggravated by Somerset's rash actions. A demagogue and an enthusiast in temper, he sympathised with the peasants and interfered personally on their behalf, issuing commissions to inquire into their grievances and promising them redress. He thus encouraged them in their opposition to the inclosure system, and inspired them with hopes which he could not satisfy.

Moreover, the debasement of the coinage resorted to by the late king had been continued and carried to still further lengths. Quantities of money of less pure metal were issued. The result was a constant and general rise in the price of commodities. By this the misery of the commonalty was deepened.

In the summer of 1549 the smouldering discontent burst out into open rebellion in the eastern counties and in the south-west. The eastern rising was entirely social and agrarian. It was directed against the inclosures. Led by Ket, a rich tanner of Wymondham, the insurgents encamped on Mousehold Hill near Norwich, and calling themselves "the king's friends and deputies" proceeded to destroy inclosures in all directions, breaking down fences and filling up ditches. In Devon and the western shires, on the other hand, there were religious grievances in addition to the agrarian and economic. The rebels there were attached to the pomp and ceremony of the old ritual, and demanded that the Latin mass should be restored, styling the new English service "a Christmas play". In the face of these revolts Somerset temporised and shrank from employing force: "he liked well the doings of the people". The lords of the Council took the matter into their own hands. Troops, including bands of foreign mercenaries, were hastily raised. The Devonshire men were overthrown at St. Mary Clyst, and the western rebellion roughly stamped out. In the east the struggle was fiercer. For a time Ket and his followers were victorious, but they were eventually crushed by Dudley, Earl of Warwick, in a bloody fight in Dussindale, beneath Mousehold Hill (August 1549). Ket and many others were executed.

Ket's rising.

To crown Somerset's difficulties came the outbreak of war with France. Henri II., who was now on the French throne, was bent on recovering Boulogne. The matter was one which might have been adjusted by firm diplomatic action, but of this the Protector was incapable. He allowed himself gradually to drift into hostilities; and when Henri, taking advantage of England's difficulties, had already captured the outlying forts of Boulogne, war was declared (September 1549).

Somerset's rule had been a failure. "He had attempted the work of a giant with the strength of a woman." He had ruined Henry's scheme of a Scottish marriage, and had involved his country in a conflict with both Scotland and France. He had pushed on religious changes with feverish haste. He had inflamed rather than calmed the social crisis. Under him the treasury had become overburdened with debt. Signs of irritation at his misgovernment had already shown themselves. His own brother Seymour of Sudleye had plotted to supplant him and been beheaded for treason (January 1549). His attitude towards the rebels finally discredited him with the lords, and in October 1549 he was deposed from the protectorate. *Somerset deposed.*

The leading place in the government was now taken by Dudley, Earl of Warwick, who later on was created Duke of Northumberland. The son of Henry VII.'s notorious minister, he had proved himself a consummate soldier and able politician. He had fought with distinction at Pinkie. He at once saw the impossibility of maintaining the struggle with France and Scotland while the exchequer was bankrupt and disorder rife in the country. He therefore procured peace, but at the cost of withdrawing the English garrisons from Scotland, and of surrendering Boulogne to Henri in return for a fraction only of the sums owed by him. *The Duke of Northumberland.*

In home affairs Northumberland's policy differed little from that of his predecessor. Fresh base money was issued by the lords of the Council, who reimbursed themselves in this way for their trouble and expenses in crushing the revolts. Trade was thrown into greater confusion than before, and prices continued to rise. Without having any religious opinions himself, it suited Northumberland's ambition to pose as the champion of the extreme reformers, who were the most active and vigorous section of the community. Altars were demolished, their places being taken by plain communion tables, and paintings were destroyed. The confiscation and pillage of church property went on as before. Livings were often kept vacant for the sake *Northumberland's Home Policy.*

of their revenues, till it was said that "there was dust on a thousand pulpits in England".

The prevailing discontent led Somerset to intrigue for the overthrow of his rival and his own return to power. His schemes were betrayed to Northumberland, and he was arrested, condemned, and executed (January 1552). To the last "this most meek and gentle duke" was beloved by the masses.

Conscious of their unpopularity, the governing clique proceeded to secure their position by means of a stringent Treason Bill. Their proposal met with a strong and unexpected opposition among the Commons, and only became law with the addition of a clause which provided that no one should be indicted for treason save on the testimony of two lawful witnesses who were to be brought face to face with the accused. This provision, though frequently evaded, proved itself "a mighty safeguard" in an age when charges of treason were easily made and difficult to meet.

In the same year (1552) the liturgical reform reached its acme. A second English Prayer Book was issued of a more reformed and progressive type than the first, and its use enforced by an Act of Uniformity. In it the dogma of transubstantiation, which had formed the philosophical basis of the privileges of the clergy, was definitely rejected. The communion became a rite commemorating Christ's sacrifice and the priest a minister. Public worship was made plain and simple, most of the pomp and show of the mediæval ritual disappearing. Shortly afterwards the Forty-two Articles were promulgated, embodying the doctrine of the church as reformed, in a liberal and comprehensive spirit. The chief share in revising the liturgy and in compiling the Articles had been taken by Cranmer, Archbishop of Canterbury. It was a task for which his broad and scholarly mind admirably fitted him.

<small>Church legislation.</small>

To alleviate the distress in the country an act was passed directing alms for the poor to be collected in every parish. It was the inauguration of a system of poor relief, which under the altered conditions was fast becoming a necessity. Northumberland too set himself to restore the finances and pay off the debts which had been contracted since Henry's death. For this purpose he wrung, although with difficulty, a subsidy from Parliament, and, as the amount was altogether insufficient, he proposed to supplement it by calling to account all who had received any money on behalf of the Crown during the last twenty years.

Meanwhile the young king, who was now fifteen years old, had been closely watching events. He was of precocious intellect. Many grammar schools bearing his name had been created out of ecclesiastical property during the reign, and at his personal instigation Christ's Hospital or the Blue Coat School had been founded for the poor children of London. Brought up amongst advanced reformers he had naturally imbibed their ideas. With the opening of 1553 his health, which had always been delicate, began to show unequivocal signs of breaking up. Northumberland was alarmed. In spite of his ability he was hated by the populace, whom he only kept down by the exercise of rigorous measures. He had given offence to all ranks of officials by his threatened inquiry into their defalcations. He had made the Princess Mary, who was next in succession to the throne, his enemy by trying to coerce her into giving up the Latin mass. Her accession meant ruin to him. Seeing Edward rapidly growing worse, he formed the ambitious design of altering the devolution of the crown and bringing it into his own family. He married his son Guildford Dudley to Lady Jane Grey, grand-daughter of Mary, Duchess of Suffolk, the younger sister of Henry VIII. Then he persuaded the dying king that he, like his father, had the right of nominating his successor, and by representing that the Reformation would be undone if Mary became queen, he induced *The will of Edward VI.* him to execute letters patent bequeathing the crown to Jane and her "heirs males". To afford further security, the leading men of the realm were compelled to sign the document. The duke was most vehement in its behalf, declaring he would "fight for it in his shirt". He opened negotiations with France for the support of a body of French troops, and equipped a fleet to intercept any help that might be sent to Mary by her cousin, the Emperor Charles V., who had more than once threatened to intervene in English affairs during the reign. The expected crisis soon arrived. On July 6th, 1553, the young king died, and the succession question came to a head.

CHAPTER VI.

THE REACTION—QUEEN MARY (1553-1558).

Northumberland's plans had been carefully laid, but treachery was at work around him. Mary was at once apprised of her brother's death, and avoided seizure by fleeing away to Framlingham, a castle of her friends the Howards, who belonged to the conservative or reactionary party in religion. Acting with true Tudor spirit, she boldly asserted her right to the throne, and appealed to the nation for support. In the meantime Jane Grey had been proclaimed queen in London by Northumberland and his allies. She was a quiet, pious girl of sixteen, highly accomplished, and deeply attached to the reformed principles. Her cause met with no favour except among the Protestant zealots, who feared to lose their ascendency. Every day that passed brought additions of strength to Mary. The fleet which Northumberland had raised went over to her side. Realising the necessity for prompt action, the duke marched from London against her, but his troops mutinied, and at Cambridge he himself was forced to declare for Queen Mary, with tears of vexation in his eyes.

Northumberland's conspiracy had failed. From the first it had been a desperate move. The duke himself was intensely unpopular, and had ruined any prospect of success he might have had by his overtures to the French for assistance. The nation was suffering acutely from the social and agrarian crisis, and was weary of the misrule of the lords, to which it attributed its miseries, and which the accession of Jane seemed likely to prolong. The religious changes had been pushed on more rapidly than the majority of the people desired. There had been much spoliation and destruction of church property. For the time the cause of reform was disgraced. Mary was the daughter of the unfortunate Catharine of Aragon, and was known to be opposed to the recent alterations in religion. She was the object of much sympathy and affection. By her father's will, which had the authorisation of Parliament, she was next entitled to the crown, and thus had on her side that strong respect for legality and legal order which exists among the English folk. *Causes of Northumberland's failure.*

The opening weeks of Mary's reign were the happiest of her life. She immediately set free the prisoners whom she found in the Tower—among them Gardiner, Edward Courtenay, and the aged Duke of Norfolk, who had narrowly escaped death for treason at the close of Henry VIII.'s reign. Courtenay was the son of the Marquis of Exeter, and had been confined in the Tower ever since the execution of his father in 1538. He was of White Rose descent, being the great-grandson of Edward IV.[1] Gardiner, who was well versed in state-craft, was made Lord Chancellor by Mary. He had formerly taken an active part in the proceedings against her mother Catharine. Throughout he had been adverse to any great reform being effected in church doctrine.

Towards those who had tried to bar her from the throne Mary showed herself unusually lenient. Lady Jane and her husband Lord Guildford Dudley were sent to the Tower. Northumberland and two of his accomplices were alone put to death. The duke's fortitude utterly gave way at the last. In the hope of being spared he abjured the reformed faith, of which he had been the champion, and whined *Execution of Northumberland.*

[1] See table on page 27.

miserably for "life, yea, the life of a dog". Endowed with splendid gifts he yet lacked the one thing which is essential for the making of a great man—principle.

In religious matters a reaction was inevitable. For many of the changes which had been carried out the popular mind was not yet ripe. This was particularly the case with the alterations in ritual and ceremonial. The masses in general preferred the pomp and external show of the old services to the simpler and purer forms of worship introduced by the English Prayer Book. The reforming party, too, had been discredited by the violence and misgovernment of its patrons. The apostasy of Northumberland, its "Joshua", fell like a thunderbolt upon it. Mary herself hated the Reformation, with which she associated the sufferings of her mother and herself. She came to the throne with the determination to undo it, and to reverse all the ecclesiastical measures of the two preceding reigns.

Without waiting for the authority of Parliament she at once, with Gardiner's assistance, set about the work. The new Prayer Book was put down and the Latin mass brought back. Foreign Protestants, Lutherans and Calvinists, who had taken refuge in England, were driven away by warnings and threats. In October, 1553, Parliament met and sanctioned the changes already in progress, by abolishing all the innovations made in the last reign and restoring ecclesiastical affairs to the condition in which they had been left by Henry VIII. The mass and the celibacy of the clergy were thus again legalised. Priests who had married were at once required to put away their wives on pain of being expelled from their cures. On this ground, or on charges of being concerned in Northumberland's conspiracy, ten prelates and nearly one-fifth of the whole body of clergy were removed. Such beginnings were ominous signs of what was to follow, and prominent members of the reform party began to withdraw to the Continent. Cranmer and Latimer, who refused to desert their posts, were committed to the Tower.

Restoration of the Mass.

The ease with which Mary had accomplished the first part of her reactionary scheme encouraged her to persevere with the remainder of it. She had already opened communications with the Roman See with a view to a reconciliation, and Cardinal Pole, who had taken the papal side against Henry VIII. and been attainted for treason, had been commissioned by the pope to proceed as legate to England. But before he could obtain leave to appear in this country, the Queen's attention became absorbed in the important question of her own marriage. *The Queen's marriage.* Her accession had been hailed with delight by her cousin, the Emperor Charles V., and from the outset she had been largely guided by his advice. His fortunes had fallen very low. He had been heavily defeated by the German Protestants, whom he had goaded into revolt by his persecutions, and he had also to face a double attack from the French and the Turks. Wishing to get control of England and her resources, he conceived the plan of marrying his son Philip to Mary. The Queen eagerly caught at the proposal. She refused to listen to the Commons when they petitioned her not to choose a foreign husband; "she would take counsel with God and with none other".

The projected marriage was highly obnoxious to the Queen's subjects. They feared that by it England would be reduced to a mere appanage or dependency of Spain, the most despotic and most intolerant power in Europe. To prevent its taking place a wide-spread conspiracy was set on foot, its leaders being extreme reformers and friends of Northumberland. Mary was to be dethroned and her place taken by her sister Elizabeth, who was to be wedded to Courtenay. Before the plot was ripe, intelligence of it came to *Rebellion of Suffolk and Wyatt.* the Chancellor's ears, and the rising was forced on prematurely (January, 1554). The Duke of Suffolk, father of Jane Grey, attempted to raise an insurrection in the Midlands, but failed, and was captured when in hiding near Coventry. It was in Kent alone that the movement assumed a formidable aspect. That shire was an advanced one, and, as in the days of Tiler and Cade, was quick to act from political motives. Assembling to the number of 15,000, the Kentishmen marched upon London under the leadership of Sir Thomas Wyatt. In the capital disaffection and dismay prevailed. The Queen, however, was "never abashed". By her courageous attitude she reanimated the loyalty of the Londoners, promising not to marry without the assent of Parliament. London Bridge was fortified against the insurgents, and Wyatt was compelled to march to Kingston to cross the Thames. His forces rapidly fell away from him. On reaching London no one rose to join him, and, after struggling on as far as Temple Bar, he surrendered with the few followers who were still left at his back (February, 1554).

"'The Queen's blood is up at last", wrote Renard, the Emperor's ambassador. Suffolk, Wyatt, and many other rebels were executed. Lady Jane Grey and Guildford Dudley, who were in imprisonment in the Tower, were sent to the block, although they had been totally unconnected with the revolt. Courtenay and Elizabeth narrowly escaped a similar fate. The immunity of jurors was not respected, a jury which acquitted Sir Nicholas Throgmorton of complicity in the rebellion being punished by the Star Chamber for its verdict.

Execution of Lady Jane Grey.

Wyatt's failure made the Spanish match a certainty. The marriage-treaty was concluded; but in it Gardiner was careful to protect English interests against aggressions on the part of Spain. Philip was to be merely titular sovereign; foreigners were not to be admitted to English offices: and England was not to be involved directly or indirectly in the war between France and the Empire. Parliament sanctioned the arrangement, and in July, 1554, Philip landed in England, and was united to Mary at Winchester. Having now the benefit of Spanish support, the Queen actively resumed her scheme for reversing the Reformation, which had been temporarily thrown into the background by her

Philip in England.

marriage. She had a considerable opposition to overcome. In November, however, a tractable Parliament was secured. Pole, who had been impatiently waiting in the Netherlands, was freed from his attainder and at once crossed over to England; and, upon the Houses promising to repeal all obnoxious legislation, he, as papal legate, absolved them and the whole realm "from heresy and schism" and reconciled them to the Roman See. In January, 1555, came the Great Bill, which swept away all the enactments which had been passed against the pope since the beginning of 1529. At the same time the persecuting Lollard Statutes were revived.

Aided by circumstances Mary had triumphed, and the papal yoke had been again imposed upon England. But the victory of the reaction was far from being perfect or complete. It had been expressly stipulated that ecclesiastical property should not be given back, but should remain in the undisturbed possession of its present owners. The Statute of Præmunire still continued on the statute-book, and Parliament refused either to restrict or define it. The Commons, too, firmly refused to allow Mary to make over the annates to the pope. The submission to Rome had been made on sufferance or extorted by surprise; whether it could be permanent events were to show. *The Reaction incomplete.*

The restoration of the papal supremacy was the signal for the outbreak of persecution. Reformed opinions were to be trampled out by force. In initiating this policy Mary and her Chancellor Gardiner were chiefly to blame. Gardiner had turned his back on his previous career. He had renounced the views he had expressed in his *De Vera Obedientia*, and had worked to put back England under the domination of the pope. The first reformer to suffer was Rogers, a prebendary of St. Paul's, who was "burnt to ashes" for not accepting the Church of Rome and its dogma of transubstantiation (February, 1555). Other burnings quickly followed, the reformers meeting death without flinching on behalf of their principles. Noticing the discontent *Persecution begins.*

produced by these measures, Philip urged the necessity of greater moderation. Already tired of a wife who was ten years older than himself, and chafing under the restraints imposed on him by Parliament, he returned in the autumn to the Continent, where his presence was needed owing to the impending abdication of Charles (1555).

After Philip's departure the persecution went on unchecked. In November Gardiner died, leaving the legate Pole as the Queen's chief counsellor. Mary, who had all a Spaniard's bigotry, was determined to extirpate "heresy" from her dominions; and "heresy" was stretched in meaning so as to cover all forms of opposition to Rome. Men were arrested and condemned for declining to recognise the pope's claim to supremacy over the English Church, or for rejecting the dogmas just formulated by the papal Council of Trent. In October, 1555, Latimer, and Ridley, the deposed Bishop of London, were burnt at Oxford. Five months later Archbishop Cranmer, whose great work had been the compilation of the English liturgy, suffered a like fate at the same place, after being arraigned and sentenced to death at Rome. The persecution was local in character. It raged with the greatest fierceness in the diocese of Canterbury, which, after Cranmer's martyrdom, had been conferred on Pole, and in the district around London, where the court had most influence. Other parts of the country were comparatively exempt. In three and a half years nearly 300 persons perished at the stake.

Martyrdom of Ridley, Latimer, and Cranmer.

The repressive policy failed in its object. The fortitude displayed by the martyrs won the admiration of the English, who are always more influenced by action than by argument. A hatred of Romanism spread on all sides. "You have lost," wrote a correspondent to Bonner, Bishop of London, who was especially distinguished for his zeal in the work of persecution, "you have lost the hearts of 20,000 that were rank papists this twelve-months." At the powerful personages

Results of the Persecution.

who were attached to Reformation principles Mary was afraid to strike. Numbers withdrew to the Continent to wait for happier times. Some of the disaffected turned pirates and plundered Spanish ships in the Channel. A plot for Mary's deposition was formed by Dudley, a cousin of Northumberland, but was detected and crushed. Much misery prevailed. The agrarian and economic crisis, which had been so prominent in the preceding reign, still lasted. It was the knowledge that Mary was slowly but surely dying that led the nation to acquiesce in the continuance of her rule.

In 1557 the struggle between France and Spain was renewed. Philip, who by the abdication of his father had become the head of the Spanish dominions, paid a hurried visit to Mary, and, in violation of the terms of their marriage-treaty, prevailed on her to ally with him against his enemies, Henri and the pope. *Loss of Calais.* This recurrence of hostilities with France brought with it fresh troubles on the Scottish border. England was ill-prepared for war. The fortifications were out of repair, and the fleet which Henry had built had been allowed to decay. An English force was sent to cooperate with the Spaniards in the north of France and was present at the capture of St. Quentin (August, 1557). After the close of the campaign the French commander, the Duke of Guise, suddenly swooped upon Calais, and in eight days captured the town (January, 1558). Calais had been the last remnant of England's possessions on the Continent; its loss was a great and humiliating blow to the national pride.

Mary's reign closed amid disaster and gloom. In November, 1558, she died. She had been Spanish rather than English in feeling. Fanatic as she was she saw that her religious policy had failed. *The Queen's death.* Her decease was followed within a few hours by that of her adviser, Pole.

CHAPTER VII.

THE RELIGIOUS SETTLEMENT—ENGLAND, SCOTLAND, AND IRELAND IN QUEEN ELIZABETH'S EARLY YEARS (1558–1568).

At Mary's death affairs were in a critical state. The realm was torn by religious dissensions. A disastrous war was on foot with France and Scotland, into which England had been drawn on behalf of Spanish interests. The treasury was empty, and there was an accumulated burden of debt. Trade was languishing. The currency was in utter confusion owing to the quantities of base coin which had been issued. The country was bankrupt, disorganised, and exhausted. The new queen, however, was a person of no ordinary capacity. The child of Henry and Anne Boleyn, Elizabeth had inherited the clear head and high imperious spirit of her father together with the vanity and coquettishness of her mother. The vicissitudes of her early life had taught her self-restraint. However strong her feelings might be, she never allowed them to get the mastery of her reason. She had the cool, calculating temper of a diplomatist. She delighted in finesse. In action she was often irresolute and vacillating, shrinking from making up her mind or taking any decisive step till the last possible moment. She had ascended the throne declaring that "nothing, no worldly thing under the sun, was so dear to her as the love and good-will of her subjects"; and to that declaration she remained true through a long reign of forty-four years. One of her first acts was to appoint William Cecil to be Secretary of State. Like Wolsey and other great ministers of this epoch, Cecil had sprung from the middle classes of society. He was a man of solid ability, sound and cautious in judgment, and of unswerving fidelity. He had already won credit as an officer of state under Henry VIII. and Edward VI.

Elizabeth and her minister at once addressed themselves

Character of Elizabeth.

to the ecclesiastical question. Many different shades of religious opinion were in existence around them. The nation as a whole had not yet split into two sects, Protestants and Roman Catholics. At one extreme was a reactionary minority who desired to main- *The Religious* tain the papal domination and the mass; and *Question in* at the other was a progressive minority who *1558.* desired to carry out far-reaching reforms, and to remould the English church according to the ideas and system of the great French reformer, Jean Calvin. Neither of these antagonistic schemes was practicable. Elizabeth took a course intermediate between the two. In January, 1559, Parliament met and passed the Acts of Supremacy and Uniformity. The Act of Supremacy re-established the independence of the national church under the crown. Sweeping away the whole of Mary's reactionary legislation, it abolished the papal and "all foreign jurisdiction" from the land, and vested the supreme authority over the church in the queen as "the only Supreme Governor of the realm as well in all spiritual or ecclesiastical things or causes as temporal". The statute also conferred large disciplinary functions upon the queen, empowering her to visit and correct heresies and ecclesiastical "contempts and enormities" and to appoint commissioners for the purpose. By virtue of the power thus given her Elizabeth shortly afterwards instituted the Court of High Commission. While the Act of Supremacy determined the government and status of the church, the Act of Uniformity settled its order of public *The* worship. The mass again disappeared, and was *Elizabethan* replaced by services in the national tongue. *Settlement.* The second Prayer Book of Edward VI. was modified in a few, but important, points where it had seemed too advanced, and its use as thus revised was strictly enjoined upon all ministers. No other form of public worship was to be used. Persons who wilfully absented themselves from church were made liable to a fine of a shilling.

The religious settlement thus effected was liberal and comprehensive. It permitted a wide freedom of opinion.

Its key-note was national independence. Although Elizabeth's supremacy differed in certain points from her father's, notably in its title of Supreme Governor instead of Supreme Head and in its narrower powers of visitation and correction, still it gave her complete control over the church and the clergy. From the nation at large she only demanded outward conformity. Everyone was required to attend church, but his conscience and belief were to be left absolutely free. Her policy in this respect closely resembled the idea of religious toleration propounded by More in his *Utopia*. Hence too it was that she deferred for the time the definite formulation of the church's creed. The Thirty-nine Articles, which were a revised form of the Forty-two Articles of Edward VI., were not promulgated and imposed on the clergy till 1571, after open war had been declared against her by Rome. For the present there was no pronounced opposition to her measures. The oath of supremacy was accepted by the vast majority of the clergy. Only about two hundred are said to have refused it, but among the number were thirteen bishops. The Marian prelates had from the first shown themselves bitterly hostile to the queen. They had even refused to crown her, and it was with difficulty that she had prevailed on Oglethorpe of Carlisle, the junior bishop of the whole bench, to place the crown upon her head. Accordingly they were all deposed. The vacant see of Canterbury was bestowed on Matthew Parker, a theologian of tolerant and enlightened opinions. He was distinguished for his knowledge of the early history of the church, and had narrowly escaped martyrdom in the Marian persecution. The other sees were filled up at the same time, partly by bringing back the exiled Edwardian bishops, partly by appointing new men whose views were known to be moderate.

Owing to the exhausted state of the kingdom it was impossible for Elizabeth to continue the war with France and Scotland. Accordingly in April, 1559, peace was signed between the three countries at Cateau Cambrésis,

Calais, England's last possession on the Continent, being left in the hands of the French. At the same time Henri and Philip also came to terms, each of them agreeing to suppress Protestantism in his own dominions. The peace of Cateau Cambrésis was an important one in history. It ended the series of French attacks upon Italy which had begun with the expedition of Charles VIII., and it marked the time at which Roman Catholicism set itself in uncompromising hostility to the Reformed faith.

Elizabeth was determined to be independent of any foreign power. By concluding peace she had freed herself from Spanish patronage, but her position was by no means secure. Her chief enemy was France. The French king "bestrode the realm, having one foot in Calais and the other in Scotland". He had gained control of the northern kingdom by marrying his son Francis to the young Scottish queen, Mary, and he hoped by means of that marriage ultimately to unite England as well as Scotland to his crown. His daughter-in-law, as the grandchild of Margaret Tudor, was by lineal descent next to Elizabeth in the English succession, and Elizabeth, the offspring of Anne Boleyn, had been stigmatised as illegitimate by the papacy. Mary and her husband had already assumed the arms of England, as though rightful sovereigns of that country. Henri, however, had a formidable opponent of his schemes in Philip. The Most Catholic King could not, in regard for his own interests, suffer Elizabeth to be overthrown by his rival. It was the perception of this fact that encouraged the English queen to persevere in her course. *Mary Queen of Scots.*

Much depended on Elizabeth's choice of a husband. Philip, in his desire to keep his hold upon England, or, as he himself phrased it, "in the service of the Lord", offered her his hand, but was refused. His relative, Charles, the Archduke of Austria, was substituted as suitor in his stead. Other wooers of the queen were the Scotch Earl of Arran, and Robert Dudley, fifth son of the late Duke of Northumberland. With respect to men, however, Elizabeth was hard *The Queen's suitors.*

to satisfy. She gravitated between her suitors according to the exigencies of her diplomacy. Her private preference was for the handsome Dudley, "sweet Robin", who owed everything to her favour, and whom later on she created Earl of Leicester. She never married.

In Scotland French predominance was complete. The regent, Mary of Guise, was supported by French troops, and governed entirely in the French interest. At Henri's direction she proceeded to put down the Reformation movement, which was rapidly spreading around her. A violent popular insurrection was the result (1559). The Scotch spirit of independence, which had been so often arrayed against the English, now turned against the French, and united with Protestant feeling in opposition to the schemes of Henri and the regent. The Lords of the Congregation, the heads of the Protestant party, appealed to Elizabeth for aid in expelling the French. The situation was a delicate one, and the queen hesitated. Just at this juncture Henri died, and was succeeded by Francis, the husband of Mary. Elizabeth at once decided to act. She secured non-intervention on the part of Spain by encouraging the suit of the Archduke Charles, while she bound the Scots more closely to her by holding out hopes to Arran. English ships and troops were sent northwards, and the French were blockaded in Leith, both by sea and land (1560). Hostilities were soon brought to a close by the Treaty of Edinburgh or Leith, which provided for the withdrawal of all French troops, and for the recognition of Elizabeth's title to the English crown. Elizabeth had gained a great victory. She had for the time destroyed French influence in the northern realm. The old national animosity against England was giving place to friendliness. In the following autumn the Scottish Reformation was completed. The authority of the pope was abjured, and the Scottish Church adopted Calvin's Confession of Faith, and was reorganised upon the Calvinistic model. Henceforward the fact that both countries were Protestant tended to draw England and Scotland more closely together.

The Treaty of Edinburgh.

Mary, who was now Queen of France as well as of Scotland, refused to ratify the Treaty of Edinburgh, or give up her pretensions to the English throne. Her uncles, the Guises, were all-powerful in France. Her position was so threatening that Elizabeth seemed likely to be forced into marrying Charles. In December, 1560, however, Francis died, and the Guises lost their influence. Mary, now a widow, returned to Scotland to pursue her schemes against Elizabeth there (1561). Bright, witty, and accomplished, she possessed the capacity of a Cleopatra for attracting and fascinating men. In conjunction with a man's vigour she had all a woman's passionate feelings, and more than a woman's power of dissimulation. *Mary returns to Scotland.* She disliked Protestantism, and was strongly attached to the Roman Church. Concealing her ambitious designs for the present, she set herself to win the loyalty of her subjects. Her influence steadily grew. The Scotch nobles, irritated at the rejection of Arran's suit, readily seconded her claim to be acknowledged as Elizabeth's successor. With such a demand the English queen could not comply. "She was not so foolish," she said, "as to hang a winding-sheet before her eyes." She saw that her recognition of Mary would merely be the prelude for an attempt on her own life by some fanatical papist.

The danger of a French attack still hung over Elizabeth. But in 1562 the first of a series of religious wars broke out in France, and that power was for the time crippled. Following her old line of policy, the English queen allied with the French Protestants or Huguenots, as they were called, just as she had formerly allied with the Scottish. She extorted from them the surrender of Havre as a pledge for the restitution of Calais. It was her aim to keep France occupied, and to prevent her enemies, the Guises, the leaders of the Roman Catholic party, from sending help to Mary. After a year's fighting a reconciliation was patched up; and as Elizabeth declined to give back Havre, the two parties united to wrest the place from her. Peace between England and France followed (1564).

Elizabeth profited by the lesson, and was careful ever afterwards, in the support she lent to the Huguenots, to avoid giving offence to French patriotism.

As the Guise influence increased in France, and as Mary felt her position growing stronger in Scotland, her tone became bolder and more confident. It was her settled ambition to secure the English throne. She never lost sight of that object. In England itself there were many Roman Catholics who regarded her as their queen by right. To get the support of Spain she proposed marrying Don Carlos, Philip's mad son, but the opposition of Elizabeth caused her to relinquish the scheme. She thereupon resolved to strengthen her position in Britain by wedding her cousin, Henry, Lord Darnley, who was descended on his father's side from the Scotch royal line, and who, moreover, stood next to herself in the English succession. Darnley, who was a mere lad of nineteen years, was a Roman Catholic. In July, 1565, he was married to Mary. Their union was a source of great alarm to Elizabeth, and to her allies, the Scotch Protestants, with whom she had maintained her friendly relations since the Treaty of Edinburgh. The leading man among them at this time was James Stuart, Earl of Moray, Mary's natural brother. Upon a promise of assistance from the English queen, Moray and Argyll took up arms, but were at once overpowered by Mary, and driven across the border into England. Elizabeth did not venture to stir. France and Spain, on whose antagonism her policy had hitherto turned, were then leagued together, and a general Roman Catholic movement against Protestantism seemed at hand. Mary looked with confidence to her co-religionists abroad for support.

Marriage of Mary and Darnley.

Mary's marriage was an ill-assorted one, and quarrels soon blazed out between her husband and herself. Darnley and his kinsmen were furious that she excluded him from all real power. Her confidence was given to David Rizzio, "a stranger Italian called Davie", through whom her intrigues with the Roman Catholic powers were carried on. A plot was formed between Darnley and the Protestant leaders, and in March, 1566, Rizzio was cruelly murdered in the very presence of the queen. Mary, however, at once broke up the confederacy. By her blandishments she won her unstable husband over to her side, and Rizzio's murderers were forced to flee for refuge to England. Her position became stronger than ever when in June she gave birth to a son, afterwards James I. In England opinion was rising in her favour. As Elizabeth did not marry, men of moderate views began to look upon her as the queen's successor. English papists crossed the frontier to pay homage to her. The Parliament, which was strongly Protestant in temper, and shrank from the prospect of a Romanist sovereign, saw the tendency of events, and urgently pressed Elizabeth to marry, and in the meantime to declare Catharine Grey her heiress-presumptive. Catharine was the grand-daughter of Mary Tudor, and by the will of Henry VIII. had been given a prior right to the crown over the Scottish line. She had, however, deeply offended Elizabeth by her clandestine marriage with Edward Seymour, son of the Protector Somerset, and her marriage had been pronounced invalid and void. So pertinacious were the Commons in their requests that the queen dissolved them in displeasure (January, 1567). Her difficulties had again led her to contemplate procuring foreign protection by marrying. Charles was still her suitor, and the preliminaries for a match with him had been actually settled. But before any binding arrangement had been made, she was released from the most pressing of her dangers by the suicidal actions of her rival.

The Scottish queen had never forgiven her husband for his share in Rizzio's murder. She was bent on revenge. Darnley had alienated his friends by his treachery; he was "sic an young fool and proud tyran". A fresh conspiracy was formed, and Darnley was murdered (February, 1567). The chief agent in the crime was the Earl of Bothwell, a fierce unscrupulous border-noble with whom Mary had become madly in-

Darnley's murder.

fatuated. She showered lands and power upon him, and finally, to the anger of the nation, married him. The lords rose in rebellion, drove Bothwell into exile, and forced Mary to abdicate and to nominate Moray as regent in the name of her son. She had ruined her prospects by her own acts. Elizabeth now felt secure. She had nothing to fear from her fallen rival, and was no longer threatened by a Roman Catholic combination in her cause. France had again been plunged into civil war, while Spain was occupied with the revolt of the Netherlands. Disliking the idea of encouraging rebellion, the English queen even refused to recognise Moray's government. Her action increased his difficulties. Mary escaped from her confinement, and rallied her friends round her, but at Langside her army was defeated, and she herself, avoiding capture, crossed as a fugitive to Carlisle (1568).

Mary flies to England.

With the flight of the Scottish queen into England the first period of Elizabeth's reign came to a close. Hitherto her great danger had lain in the enmity of Mary and of France; and against that she had guarded herself by allying with the Scotch Protestants and French Huguenots, and by cultivating amicable relations with Philip, either directly, or else indirectly through her marriage negotiations with his kinsman, Charles. The centre of peril now changed. In the future the queen's foes were to be the papacy and Spain, and their hostility was to culminate finally in the decisive crisis of the Armada.

The ten years that had passed had been years of progress. England had grown stronger, more settled, more united. The government was wise and economical. The currency had been reformed, and the national credit restored. The impure coin issued in the preceding reigns had been called in to the mint, and its place taken by fresh money of standard quality (1560). Trade and commerce were fast growing. The queen's religious settlement had commended itself to the bulk of the nation. Although neither Romanists nor Calvinists might be satisfied, still as yet no declared hostility had shown itself.

And in Ireland the turbulent Shane O'Neill had been suppressed, and better peace and order attained.

At the opening of the Tudor epoch Ireland had presented a scene of anarchy and disorder. The Pale, as that part of the country was termed where the king's writ ran and English law was administered, had shrunk to the narrowest dimensions. In length it extended merely from Dundalk to a few miles south of Dublin, while its average width was barely twenty miles. Outside this restricted area the barbarous "Brehon" laws prevailed, which recognised common or tribal ownership of land and allowed murder to be atoned for by a money payment. Under such a system bloodshed was of everyday occurrence. Whole districts paid tribute to native chiefs, who oppressed and pillaged at will. There was no national or racial union. Between the various families and septs bitter and interminable feuds raged. The descendants of the Anglo-Norman barons who had settled in the island had sunk into Irish chieftains, and adopting the native manners and customs had "become more Irish than the Irish themselves". The towns alone formed an exception to the general anarchy. {*Ireland under the Tudors.*}

What Ireland needed was to be thoroughly and systematically subjugated. But the first Tudor monarch was far too insecurely seated on the throne to attempt such a task. He resorted therefore to the easier plan of ruling the country by means of the most powerful of the Anglo-Norman families, and with this object he chose as Lord Deputy the Earl of Kildare, the head of the northern branch of the Fitzgeralds or Geraldines. The Earl soon proved faithless to his trust, giving assistance to Simnel and afterwards intriguing with Warbeck. He was in consequence deposed, and an Englishman, Sir Edward Poynings, put in his place (1494). {*Poynings' Law.*}

For the moment a stronger policy was adopted. The parliament which was held at Drogheda passed the so-called Poynings' Acts, by which the Irish legislature was made directly dependent upon the crown. They directed that for the future no Irish parliament should be summoned unless the king had first been informed of the measures to be laid before it and had approved of them. The Poynings' Acts regulated the constitutional relations of the two countries for nearly three centuries. As the danger from the "White Rose" pretender vanished, Henry reverted to his former course and reinstated Kildare as Deputy. "If all Ireland cannot rule him," he said, "then he shall rule all Ireland." His confidence was abused. Instead of maintaining order Kildare engaged in a number of wars against his private enemies, representing that they were for the benefit of the crown. He was at chronic feud with the Butlers, whose leader was the Earl of Ormonde. His son Gerald, who succeeded him as Deputy (1513), followed in his footsteps. The fighting and raiding between the different clans went on unchecked until in 1520 Gerald was superseded, and an English governor, the Earl of Surrey, sent across. Surrey had the instincts of a soldier, and at once set about reducing the island to submission. He captured the castle of the O'Connors and enacted loyalty from the Southern or Desmond Geraldines. But finding himself inadequately supported by Henry VIII., whose interest was centred in continental affairs, he procured his own recall. The plan of using an Anglo-Norman family to govern Ireland was again employed, and Gerald of Kildare was again selected for the post (1522). Turbulent and vindictive like his father, he prosecuted his family feuds without intermission. Under him the hostility between his own house, the Geraldines, and that of the Butlers grew more vehement than ever. In consequence of the prevailing disorder, Sir William Skeffington was appointed in 1527 to act as governor of the island. But the resources placed at his disposal were limited, and he could effect little or nothing. Kildare set his authority at defiance, attacking the Butlers, the O'Donnells, and other rival clans, and eventually securing his own reappointment as Deputy (1532). He again made use of his official position to attack his personal enemies "using the sword utterly to extinguish the fame and honour of any noble within that land, shadowed with that authority so that whatever he did should not be repugned at". Owing to his raids Dublin was reduced to a state bordering on starvation. He even carried off the royal artillery to his own castles. His offences at last became so flagrant that he was summoned to England and thrown into the Tower (1534). The Geraldines and their numerous dependants at once rose in revolt under his son Offaly. The Pale was invaded and ravaged by the rebels, and Dublin Castle besieged. Fortunately for Henry the Butlers remained loyal. Still the danger was serious. The emperor and the pope were at the time threatening an attack upon England, and Offaly made overtures for an alliance with them, offering to hold Ireland as their vassal. Charles promised to send him assistance, but before any came the rising had been crushed. Skeffington, who had again been placed at the head of affairs, captured Maynooth Castle, the stronghold of the Geraldines, and hanged twenty-six out of the thirty-seven prisoners who fell into his hands (1535). This rigorous act, "the pardon of Maynooth", broke the back of the rebellion. Offaly surrendered, and was executed at Tyburn with five of his uncles (1537). The ascendency of the Northern Geraldines was gone for ever.

Rebellion of the Geraldines.

The Geraldine revolt inaugurated a more vigorous policy on the part of the English government. The old method of ruling Ireland with the help of the most powerful of the Anglo-Norman clans was abandoned. Lord Leonard Grey was created Deputy, and, after stamping out the remnants of the rebellion, began a series of expeditions against the wild native tribes. His energetic measures caused the Irish lords to become alarmed for their independence, and an extensive confederacy was formed centring round Gerald, the dispossessed heir of Kildare. It comprised alike the O'Neill of the north and the Desmond of the south. There was, too, a papal or religious element in the outbreak. Henry had become the head of the Irish Church as well as of the English, and priests journeyed from chief to chief urging them "for God's sake and the salvation of their souls" to fight against the "heretic" who had abolished the pope's supremacy. An army of northern rebels burst into the Pale, but was overtaken and crushed by Grey at Bellahoe, on the northern border of Meath (1539). This victory shattered the confederacy. The king's rule had never before been such a reality in Ireland as now.

Victories of Lord Grey.

The Reformation merely added a fresh source of disturbance to the island. The condition of the Irish Church was a scandal to Christendom. In no other country were the clergy so lazy, ignorant, and degraded. "There was no archbishop nor bishop, abbot nor prior, parson nor vicar nor any other that used to preach the Word of God, saving the poor friars beggars." But in spite of the gross abuses which prevailed there was no demand for ecclesiastical reform. The government's measures, copied from the acts of the English parliament, were at the most not resisted; they were never desired. Henry acquired the supremacy over the Irish Church; the papal jurisdiction was abrogated; and the property of monasteries and religious houses was confiscated. Changes in ritual corresponding to those in England were also established by law; but in practice very little was done towards actually carrying them out.

As the resistance of the native tribes had been broken, Henry fell back upon a conciliatory line of action. In 1541 he raised Ireland, which had hitherto been merely a lordship, to the rank of a kingdom, thus placing it on an equality with England in point of dignity. It was his aim to convert the chiefs into English nobles, and by their agency to spread English law and English civilisation throughout the island. Efforts were made to induce them to submit to hold their lands of the king, to abjure the pope, and to have their sons educated at the English court. This policy, quietly persisted in, soon began to bear fruit. Clan

Henry's conciliatory policy.

after clan sent in its submission. Grants of ecclesiastical lands and presents helped on the process. O'Neill was created Earl of Tyrone, and O'Brien Earl of Thomond. Much, too, was effected by the prudence and diplomacy of the Deputy, St. Leger. He saw the danger of forcing the Irish chiefs into an alliance with foreign powers, and so preferred "to use gentleness to such as showed themselves conformable". In religious matters his administration was particularly tolerant. When the council under Edward VI., striving after an absolute uniformity between the two countries, imposed the English Prayer-book on Ireland in the place of the mass, he declined to take steps to compel its use where the Irish did not understand English. To the reforming enthusiasts, who were then in power, he appeared "a dissimular in religion", and was recalled to make way for a man more after their own heart.

The accession of Mary brought with it a reaction in religious matters in Ireland, just as in England. Her reign too saw the commencement of the policy of colonisation, which was fated in after-times to prejudice vitally the quiet reduction of the country to law and order. The territories of the O'Connors and O'Mores, situated in central Ireland, were confiscated by the government and sold or transferred to English settlers. *The Marian Plantation.* In the confiscation the land was treated as the absolute property of the chief, no regard being paid to the rights which by Brehon law were possessed by the members of the sept. There followed in consequence a fierce and protracted guerrilla warfare between the disinherited tribesmen and the colonists. Fresh schemes of "plantation" were in the air when Elizabeth came to the throne, but Cecil in his caution rejected them. The example, however, had been set, and an uneasy feeling prevailed among the Irish septs. It was for this reason that the rising of Shane O'Neill became so formidable.

The death of O'Neill, Earl of Tyrone, gave the signal for a fresh dispute. The English and Irish laws of succession came into conflict. According to the former

Matthew, the Earl's eldest son, was his next successor; but by Celtic custom the sept had a limited power of election, and proceeded to choose a younger son, Shane, as its head. Shane acted with characteristic vigour. He assassinated his rival, and summoning his clansmen to his standard, defeated the Deputy Sussex in a fight near Armagh (1561). The English government, being already surrounded with difficulties at home, shrank from a war in Ireland. Shane visited London, and was acknowledged as Captain of Tyrone and Antrim upon certain conditions. These conditions he immediately set at nought on his return. He overthrew the Scots of Antrim and invaded Connaught. On all sides he acted cruelly and despotically. It was his ambition to make himself supreme over the north, if not over the whole of Ireland. With great reluctance Elizabeth at length realised the necessity of suppressing him. Her lieutenant, Sir Henry Sidney, drew together a league of northern chiefs who had been wronged by the tyrant. Attacked and defeated by the O'Donnells, "Shane the Proud" fled from before the approach of Sidney's forces, and shortly afterwards perished in an obscure skirmish (1566). After his death a state of comparative quiet prevailed for a time. The next serious disturbance was caused by Roman Catholic intrigues.

[margin: Shane O'Neill.]

CHAPTER VIII.

THE STRUGGLE WITH SPAIN AND THE PAPACY (1568–1588).

Elizabeth, like the other members of the Tudor line, was a strong upholder of the principle of authority. She disliked the notion of aiding or encouraging subjects who were in rebellion against their lawful sovereign. It was this feeling which had prevented her from directly supporting the Scotch nobles and recognising the regency of her ally Moray, just as in later years it prevented her from giving consistent help to the Dutch patriots. At first it was her idea to restore the fugitive Mary to the Scottish throne, but under such conditions as would render her powerless for future mischief. She accordingly appointed a commission of lords to inquire into the late revolution in Scotland; and before them Moray, in justifying his line of action, produced the famous Casket Letters,[1] which (if genuine) clearly established Mary's complicity in the murder of Darnley. Elizabeth at once saw that her restoration was impossible, while Mary on her side emphatically refused to confirm her abdication or Moray's title as regent. The inquiry, which had damaged Mary in the eyes of Europe, was hushed up. Moray was sent back to Scotland with a supply of money, while his sister remained in honourable captivity in England, to become the centre of conspiracies against Elizabeth's life and throne. Mary's defiant attitude was not without reason. Enchanted by the concourse of northern gentry to her side at Carlisle, she had come to believe that her party in England was as strong as that of the Queen herself. She had, moreover, a prospect of getting Spanish aid, serious differences having arisen between the English sovereign and Philip.

<small>Mary remains in England.</small>

Those differences were partly religious and partly commercial. The Spanish government was bigotedly Roman Catholic, and had entered on a policy of crushing Protestant or Reforming doctrines by force. Its religious intolerance and its contempt for popular liberties had provoked insurrectionary movements in the Netherlands, which Alva, Philip's viceroy, was putting down with atrocious severity. There was much sympathy in England for the oppressed Netherlanders, many of whom began to cross to this country for refuge. In the Channel English and Flemish rovers abounded, who seized and plundered Spanish ships as they passed to and from the insurgent provinces. Their

<small>Differences with Spain.</small>

---

[1] These letters are supposed to be the correspondence between Mary and Bothwell. Their authenticity has been doubted by some historians.

bitterness against Spain was intensified by the fact that English sailors were constantly seized by the authorities of that land and handed over to the Holy Inquisition to be imprisoned or burnt as heretics. In the American seas too collisions took place. The Most Catholic King, by virtue of a bull of Pope Alexander VI., claimed nearly the whole New World as his exclusive possession, and strove by forcible measures to put an end to the visits which English mariners had begun to pay to those quarters. The chief offender against his monopoly was John Hawkins, who was the first Englishman to engage in the slave-trade between Africa and the American colonies. The friendship between the English and Spanish governments which had prevailed during the early years of the reign was already at an end when, in December, 1569, Elizabeth seized a quantity of money which Philip had borrowed from Genoese merchants for the payment of Alva's troops in the Netherlands. This high-handed act nearly led to a war. Cecil, foreseeing that a struggle with papal and aggressive Spain was ultimately inevitable, was eager that the queen should boldly and fearlessly accept the position of leader of Protestant Europe. Such a decided course did not commend itself to Elizabeth; she was adverse to bloodshed, and preferred to employ the peaceful subtleties of diplomacy. Philip on his side was not prepared for war, and submitted to the affront which had been put upon him. Henceforward his hostility to Elizabeth increased, and he began gradually and tentatively to espouse the cause of Mary, her enemy.

The quarrel with Spain indirectly brought on an outbreak of rebellion in England. For some time various elements of discontent had been gathering, particularly in the northern shires, where the partisans of Mary, and the adherents of the old or unreformed creed and worship, were most numerous. There was also in aristocratic circles a wide-spread dislike of the ascendency of Cecil, a "new man". A scheme was formed for overthrowing him and replacing him by the Duke of Norfolk, who was to be married to the Scottish queen. Norfolk was the son of the brilliant but rash Earl of Surrey, who had incurred the penalties of treason at the close of Henry VIII.'s reign. In the face of Elizabeth's opposition the plan collapsed, and upon the duke's disloyally renewing his intrigues he was committed to the Tower. In the retrograde north, the traditional source of rebellion against the Tudors, the disaffection took a more desperate form. Stirred up by a papal agent, the northern malcontents aimed at dethroning the queen in favour of her rival Mary, who was to be wedded to Don Juan, natural brother of Philip, and at re-establishing the unreformed worship and Roman supremacy. They negotiated with Alva for the support of a detachment of Spanish troops. At their head were the Earls of Northumberland and Westmoreland, the representatives of the powerful families of the Percies and the Nevills. In November, 1569, the two earls prematurely rose in rebellion, seized Durham, where they tore up the English Bible and Prayerbook and celebrated mass, and marched upon Tutbury, to secure the person of the Scottish queen. Mary, however, was removed out of their reach to Coventry. Their followers fell away; no aid came to them from Alva; and they were soon forced to flee across the border into Scotland. The revolt, which had been aristocratic in complexion, was punished with great severity. It was the first and the only real rebellion that troubled the reign of Elizabeth. Cecil was more influential than before, and not long after was created Lord Burghley (1571).

<small>The Rising in the North.</small>

The rising was followed by a declaration of war against Elizabeth on the part of Rome. The pope, Pius V., who had distinguished himself as an Inquisitor, was fiercely bent on extirpating the Reformation in any and every shape. He regarded England as the chief centre of "the venom". He had helped to stir up the northern rebellion, and in February, 1570, before its complete collapse was known, he issued a bull excommunicating Elizabeth, "the heretic, pretended Queen of England, servant of iniquity", and

<small>Elizabeth excommunicated.</small>

depriving her of her crown. Her subjects were released from their allegiance, and forbidden to obey her under pain of excommunication. The papal fulmination marked a turning-point in the religious history of the reign. Hitherto the Queen's government had been marked by great tolerance: there had been practically no persecution. As long as dissentients outwardly conformed and attended church, they were not interfered with. Pius's bull rendered the continuance of this tolerant policy impossible. It drew for the first time a hard-and-fast line between Romanists and Protestants, and identified Romanism with disloyalty. Inculcating treason as a duty, it made it impracticable for a Papist to be true both to his country and to his religion. It forced the English government to take measures in self-defence, and thus led to the enactment of a series of penal statutes against Roman Catholics.

Since the beginning of the reign Protestantism had made great progress in the country. The doctrines of Calvin, the Genevan reformer, had spread on every hand. There was a constantly increasing number of "Puritans" whom the Queen's religious settlement did not satisfy, and who wished to reform the Church still further, and make it more nearly resemble the Calvinistic type. The Parliament, which was convened in the spring of 1571 to answer Pius's bull, was strongly Protestant in temper. It met the pope's pretensions and Mary's claims by affirming the Queen's title to the crown, and making it high treason to declare her "a heretic" or "a usurper". It passed an act forbidding under the severest penalties anyone to "obtain, publish, and put in use" papal bulls and other instruments within the realm, or to absolve subjects from their allegiance, and reconcile them to the "usurped authority" of the Roman see. At the same time, to guard against disloyalty within the Church itself, it made assent to the teaching of the Thirty-nine Articles obligatory upon the clergy.

Anti-Papal legislation.

The Papal anathema encouraged the intrigues of Mary and her partisans, and gave rise to a series of conspiracies against the person and sceptre of the English queen. The first of these, the Ridolfi plot, was con- **The Ridolfi** nected with the same disaffection as had pro- **Plot.** duced the northern revolt. The prime mover in it was Ridolfi, a Florentine banker, who passed to and fro between the English malcontents, Mary, Alva in the Netherlands, the Roman pontiff, and Philip. Through his agency a conspiracy was set on foot for imprisoning or murdering Elizabeth, and placing Mary on the throne with the help of Spanish troops. The Most Catholic King and the Pope entered warmly into the scheme, the latter declaring himself "ready to sell even the chalices from the churches" in its behalf. The plotters, however, did not long escape the vigilance of Burghley, and in September 1571 the whole conspiracy was laid bare. Norfolk, who had been implicated in it, was tried, condemned, and after some delay, upon the repeated demands of the Commons was executed (1572). **Execution of** Traitorous, unstable, and hypocritical, he **Norfolk.** richly deserved his fate. Throughout he had been professedly a Protestant. Parliament, in its alarm, was eager to attaint the Scottish queen of treason, but to this Elizabeth would not consent. Relying on the loyalty of her subjects, and ignorant of personal fear, she steadily refused, both now and afterwards, to take any exceptional measures for her own protection. After a short period of closer confinement Mary was left as free to carry on her intrigues as before.

For some time the relations between England and France had been growing more friendly. As Spanish hostility to her developed, Elizabeth had naturally turned towards France, Spain's great rival, just as she had formerly looked to Spain in opposition to Henri II.'s schemes. Friendship with France became the cornerstone of her foreign policy. The position of affairs in that realm was favourable to her. The queen- **The French** mother, Catharine de' Medici, had a strong **Alliance.** dislike of Mary Stuart, and was little inclined to second her ambition. A temporary close had been put to the religious war by the peace of St. Germain (1570). The Guises, the relatives of Mary and the heads of the papal and Spanish party, had lost their commanding influence, which had passed to Coligny, the Huguenot leader, and Coligny was eager for a league with England against the common enemy Spain. The only obstacle in the way was Scotland. The French could not forget that the Stuarts had formerly been their compliant allies, and, by way of upholding French interests, constantly sent supplies of money to the adherents of Mary in their contest with the Regent Moray. In January, 1570, Moray, who had been steadily true to the English connection, was assassinated. His death so greatly weakened the young king's party that Elizabeth found it necessary to send it some military assistance. Negotiations, too, were opened between herself and the French king, Charles IX., for a joint settlement of the Scottish question. Their intercourse grew still more amicable when, at Elizabeth's prompting, Charles' brother, the Duke of Anjou, afterwards Henri III., offered himself as a suitor for her hand. She had suggested the match merely in order to prevent any alliance between the duke and Mary, and, when that end had been attained, it was quietly allowed to drop. Events on the Continent completed the friendly understanding between the English and French courts. The annihilation of the Turkish fleet at Lepanto (1571) made Philip absolutely supreme in the Mediterranean. Charles was alarmed at his rival's increase of power, and in April, 1572, entered into a defensive alliance with the English queen.

The strength of the alliance thus concluded was soon tested by two important events, the revolt of the Netherlands and the massacre of St. Bartholomew, which both occurred in the same year (1572). For some time Philip's viceroy, Alva, had been exercising in the Low Countries a tyranny of the worst description. His merciless persecution of the Protestants drove thousands of peaceful artisans to flee for refuge to other lands. Many of them, like their

Alva in the Low Countries.

predecessors in the reign of Edward III., settled in England, particularly in the eastern counties and Kent, where they introduced new species of manufacture, notably the weaving of improved kinds of cloth. Their immigration was of immense benefit to the English woollen trade. In the opening months of 1572 a band of Dutch refugees, led by William de la Marck, suddenly seized the town of Brille, situated on an island at the mouth of the Maas. This action, which was altogether unpremeditated, had important consequences: it proved the first step in the foundation of the United Netherlands, now generally known as Holland. Many of the cities of the Low Countries at once revolted against Alva's government, and put themselves under the rule of William, Prince of Orange, as Stadtholder of King Philip. French help was sent to the insurgents, and Charles made eager proposals to Elizabeth for a joint attack upon Philip and a partition of the insurgent provinces between the Queen and himself. His plan was too far-reaching for her liking, and was declined. Fresh schemes of combined action in the Netherlands were being discussed by the two sovereigns when the massacre of St. Bartholomew took place (August, 1572). At the instigation of Catharine de' Medici and the Guises, numbers of French Protestants, variously estimated at 25,000 and at 100,000, were ruthlessly butchered. Coligny and the other leaders were amongst the slain. The Huguenot ascendency at the French court was destroyed at a blow. Never afterwards was there a possibility of France becoming a Protestant state. The Most Catholic King laughed for joy, and the pope, "the Vicar of Christ", held a solemn thanksgiving to God for the hideous slaughter.[1] In England the alarm was great. For the moment it seemed that a league for the extirpation of Protestantism was in existence between the Roman Catholic powers, and an instant attack was feared. The cordiality just established with the French court ceased.

The Massacre of St. Bartholomew.

---

[1] Large frescoes representing the murder of Coligny, and other incidents of the slaughter, still adorn one of the ante-rooms of the Vatican.

On the state of affairs in the Netherlands the massacre had an immediate influence. It had thrust France again into the chaos of a religious war. No French aid was now forthcoming to the insurgents. Alva captured town after town, barbarously putting the inhabitants to death. Elizabeth foresaw great danger to herself if the Spaniards subjugated the Netherlands, and was led in her own defence to interfere on behalf of the Dutch. She sent money to the Prince of Orange, and encouraged English volunteers to cross to his support. At the same time she despatched Hawkins westwards to intercept the treasure-fleet which was bringing the produce of the American mines to Spain. Before long the outlook brightened. Alva's ferocity stiffened the resistance of the patriots, who, by cutting the dykes and laying their country under water, forced his troops to withdraw. Having failed to achieve his object by severity, he retired from his command (1573). His successor, Requesens, followed a more moderate and pacific policy.

While France was occupied with the civil war kindled by the massacre of St. Bartholomew, Elizabeth seized the opportunity to effect a settlement of affairs in Scotland. *Affairs of Scotland.* Through her mediation the chief supporters of Mary were induced to submit to the Regent Morton, and an English force under Drury forced the remainder, who were holding Edinburgh Castle, to surrender (1573). Mary's party in Scotland thus ceased to exist, and the authority of Morton, who was a friend of the English government, was recognised on every hand.

As the panic created by the slaughter of the Huguenots died away, the friendship between Elizabeth and the court of Paris was gradually restored. Her relations with Spain too became less hostile after Alva's retirement, *Don Juan of Austria and his plans.* commercial intercourse between the two countries being resumed. This improvement, however, soon ceased when Don Juan of Austria, the versatile and brilliant half-brother of Philip, arrived as governor of the Netherlands (1576). The victor of Lepanto and the darling of the pope, who had hailed him as "a man sent from God whose name was John", it was the ambition of Juan to seize England for himself and the Roman see. He meant, after speedily reducing the insurgent provinces, to attack Elizabeth, seat himself and Mary Stuart on the English throne, and suppress Protestantism. His scheme had the warm approval of Gregory XIII., the Roman pontiff. He quickly found that his task in the Netherlands was one that taxed all his energies. The brutal sack of Antwerp by the Spanish soldiery had led all the provinces, Roman Catholic as well as Protestant, to make common cause together for the vindication of their liberties and the expulsion of foreign troops. Don Juan saw himself obliged to dismiss the Spanish army with which he had hoped to invade England. His treacherous conduct soon provoked a fresh outbreak of hostilities; and the States appealed to both England and France for aid. Seeing the need of thwarting her enemy's plans, Elizabeth supported the Dutch with a large loan, and subsidised the Count Palatine to lead a German army to their assistance. She also hampered Philip's action by letting loose English privateers against the colonies and shipping of Spain. With her sanction Francis Drake, a kinsman of Hawkins, sailed to the South Pacific, where he inflicted enormous damage on the Spaniards. Having collected a rich booty he returned home round the Cape of Good Hope, thus circumnavigating the world. *Drake in the Pacific.* Don Juan never made his projected attempt upon England. He died in the autumn of 1578, leaving the Low Countries still unsubdued. His successor was Alessandro Farnese, Duke of Parma, who was the finest general of the age.

For some time a Counter-Reformation or Roman Catholic reaction had been in progress in Europe. The impulse of the Reformation seemed to have spent itself. The Roman Church had undergone a process of regeneration, and had set itself resolutely to recover the ground which had been lost. Its dogmas had been rigidly defined by the Council of Trent. It had powerful instruments at its command in the newly-founded order of Jesuits and the Inquisition. If these proved insufficient for its purpose, it made use alike of open force and of assassination, calling in the temporal princes to its aid. The Most Catholic King was its "sword-arm". It had crushed out of existence the Protestant movements in Southern Europe. The massacre of St. Bartholomew had dealt Huguenotism a heavy blow. England, which was looked **The Romanist attack.** upon as the bulwark of the Protestant world, was now to be assaulted. During the years which followed the advent of Don Juan in the Netherlands, Elizabeth had to encounter the full force of the Counter-Reformation. The attack, as planned by the pope, the Duke of Guise, and the Jesuits, took a threefold form. Simultaneous attempts were made in Scotland, in Ireland, and in England itself.

In Scotland the extreme youth of the king, James VI., afforded an opening for intrigue. The Jesuit plan was to get control of him, effect his conversion to the Roman Catholic faith, and involve him in a war with England, in **Scottish affairs.** which a combined French and Scottish force would cross the border, overthrow Elizabeth, and set his mother Mary on the throne. The agent sent to carry out this scheme was Esmé Stuart, a young Scotch noble, who had been brought up in France. Esmé speedily won the favour of James, who had just been declared of age, and who created him Duke of Lennox. By his craft he contrived to bring Morton, the mainstay of the Protestant and English party, to the scaffold. But there his success ended. Philip was far too deeply engaged in the Netherlands and Portugal to provide him with an armed force. His proceedings aroused the strong Protestant feeling of the Scots, and in August, 1582, a band of lords, who favoured the English connection, seized possession of James and of the government (Raid of Ruthven). Lennox's scheming came to light, and he was compelled to flee to France. The Roman Catholic attempt in Scotland had utterly failed. A little later (1586) Elizabeth, by means of a moderate pension, secured the good-will of James, who was already fixing his hopes on the English succession. Henceforward she had nothing to fear on the side of Scotland.

Ireland presented a promising field for an attack upon the English queen. Since the fall of Shane O'Neill there had been no extensive revolt in the island, but its condition was far from settled. The Queen in her parsimony starved her Irish government. Her deputies were left unsupported, and were unable to enforce law and order. Her garrisons were few in number and badly paid, the soldiers being often compelled for want of supplies to live at free quarters among the people. Moreover, schemes of colonisation, which were being continually mooted, kept up a restless spirit among the Irish. Already in the last reign the lands of the O'Mores and O'Connors in Leinster had been planted with English settlers. In 1573 an attempt was made by the Earl of Essex to colonise the district of Clandeboy, to the north of Lough Neagh in Antrim, but the hostility of the neighbouring septs caused it to fail. Plans were also set on foot for establishing English proprietors in parts of Munster which had been confiscated. These and similar proposals filled the Irish with suspicion against the English government. The ground was thus prepared for Roman Catholic intrigues. There was, however, little religious discontent. Elizabeth's ecclesiastical settlement in Ireland had been similar to that in England. The Acts of Supremacy and Uniformity applied to both countries equally, but in Ireland, although not resisted, they remained practically a dead letter. The English Prayer-book, which was as unintelligible to the natives as the Latin mass, was little used. Religious and sectarian animosity had scarcely yet arisen. *Irish affairs.*

For some time English and Irish refugees had been urging Philip and the pope to attack Elizabeth in Ireland. Papal emissaries had already been sent to stir up the latent disaffection. In 1579 Fitz-maurice, brother of Desmond, who had already been concerned in treasonable practices against the government, and Sanders, a Roman legate, landed in Kerry *Rebellion in Ireland.*

with a commission from the pope. Their arrival was the signal for a revolt, in which Desmond and most of the southern chiefs took part. Youghal was taken and sacked. A fierce spasmodic warfare ensued, which was marked by massacres and wholesale ravages on both sides. Fitzmaurice perished in a skirmish. The imposition of a tax for the maintenance of the English forces caused the insurrection to blaze out afresh among the barons of the Pale; and the army of the Deputy, Lord Grey de Wilton, was entrapped and defeated at Glenmalure in the Wicklow Hills (1580). This disaster, and the landing of 800 Spanish and Italian troops, drove Elizabeth to act for the moment with greater vigour. Smerwick, where the invaders had intrenched themselves, was forced by Grey to surrender, and its garrison put to the sword. Its fall ensured the collapse of the revolt, which was gradually localised by the English generals, and stamped out with great severity. Desmond was betrayed and killed (1583). Large districts of Munster were confiscated by the government, and passed into the hands of English owners. The Roman Catholic attack in Ireland had resulted in failure. The country was for the time cowed, and when, a few years later, Philip sent his Armada against England, not a single Irish chieftain ventured to stir in his support.

Desmond's Rebellion quelled.

The direct assault upon England, which was made by the papal party simultaneously with their intrigues in Scotland and Ireland, was half-religious, half-political in character. The most ardent of the English Romanists had already withdrawn across the Channel to the Continent. One of them, an Oxonian named William Allen, had, in 1568, founded a college at Douai in Flanders for educating young Englishmen, and training them for mission work in their native land. From the year 1574 onwards, Allen's Seminarists had begun to arrive in England. Their efforts to extend the Roman Catholic faith and overthrow the Elizabethan Settlement did not meet with such rapid success as Allen had hoped, and in 1579 he enlisted the support of the

The Jesuits in England.

powerful and aggressive order of Jesuits in the cause. By way of seconding the labours of Esmé Stuart in Scotland and Sanders in Ireland, a regular Jesuit mission, under Campion and Parsons, was, in 1580, despatched to this country. Its object was not religious merely. It was intended to carry out the policy of the bull of deposition by fomenting discontent, and preparing the way for a foreign invasion for the establishment of Roman Catholicism. The effect of the preaching of the Seminarists and Jesuits was soon seen. Many Roman Catholics, who had hitherto outwardly conformed and attended the English service, ceased to do so. Their dislike of the Queen's ecclesiastical laws deepened into hostility. Recusancy, or non-attendance at church, grew more frequent. The government saw the success of its religious policy threatened by the missionaries, and in 1581 a statute was passed which increased the fine for recusancy from one shilling to £20 a month, and imposed the penalties of treason on anyone who should convert any of the Queen's subjects to "the Romish religion", or induce them to promise obedience to the See of Rome. A sharp persecution of the Romanist missionaries now began, Campion himself being arrested and executed as a traitor. **The Recusancy Laws.**

Meanwhile Elizabeth had again been brought to the verge of marriage. Left to themselves the Netherlanders had been unable to make head against Parma, and the southern or Roman Catholic provinces had chosen the Duke of Alençon, brother of Henri III., to be their protector. Elizabeth saw the danger of a French annexation of the Low Countries, and set herself to gain a hold upon the duke, and force him to act as she wished. He had already been suggested for her hand. She now took up the proposal with eagerness. Alençon was invited to England, and in spite of his dwarfish stature and repulsive appearance, the Queen, who was twenty years his senior, professed to find him charming. The conquest of Portugal by Philip (1580), and the despatch of fresh Spanish troops to the Netherlands, **The Alençon Marriage.**

threw the English and French courts still closer together. A treaty of marriage with Alençon was concluded, the Queen inciting him to attack Parma, and furnishing him with funds for the purpose. In the following year (1581) the revolted princes declared themselves severed from Spain, and with the exception of Holland and Zeeland, which clung to William, Prince of Orange, accepted Alençon as their sovereign. The duke, however, chafed under the constitutional restraints put upon him, and tried by a coup d'état to make himself absolute. All confidence between him and his subjects was destroyed; the Spaniards took city after city; and in 1583 he retired to France to die. Elizabeth had never really meant to wed him. By encouraging his suit she had kept him and his brother Henri from siding with Spain and the Guises, and had, without cost to herself, caused Philip to be resisted in the Netherlands.

After Alençon's disappearance Parma, taking advantage of the religious differences among the insurgents, and having the vigorous support of the Jesuits, gradually recovered the Romanist provinces of the south for his master. The northern and Protestant districts organised themselves into a republic under William of Orange and proclaimed their independence. Shortly afterwards the prince, whom Philip had branded as "an enemy of the human race", and on whose head he had put a price, was shot dead by a Roman Catholic assassin (1584).

Parma reconquers Belgium.

In England the Jesuit mission had fired the fanaticism of the extreme Romanists. Several conspiracies against the Queen followed in succession. In December, 1583, the Throgmorton plot was discovered. It had aimed at assassinating Elizabeth and putting Mary on the throne with the help of Spain. Mendoza, the Spanish ambassador, had been concerned in it, and was expelled. The murder of Orange showed the reality of the peril to which the Queen was exposed. As she declined to take any precautionary measures herself, her councillors and chief nobles drew up a Voluntary

Throgmorton's Plot.

Bond of Association for her protection (1585). The Bond was a direct warning to Mary. Shortly afterwards it received the sanction of Parliament, which further provided that if a plot should be formed against the queen "by or with the privity of anyone pretending title to the crown", such person should be tried by an extraordinary commission of lords and judges. In the same session an act was passed expelling all Jesuits and Roman Catholic priests from the realm, and forbidding English children to be educated in Romanist seminaries abroad. For some years, while the alarm lasted, the Roman Catholics were rigorously treated. The penal laws enacted against them were put in force. Not a few of the Romanist missionaries were put to death, Burghley declaring that they were punished, not for religion, but for treason.

Circumstances soon brought Elizabeth into open antagonism with the Spanish king. In 1585 the Roman Catholic League, formed by the Guises and Philip, became predominant in France, and by compelling Henri III. to proscribe the Protestant worship, caused a fresh war of religion to break out. The French alliance, on which Elizabeth had relied in her duel with the Spanish monarch, was thus lost to her. In the Netherlands, too, the assassination of Orange, her friend, had dealt a heavy blow to the cause of the Dutch. She saw herself forced to take a more pronounced course in their support. Declining the sovereignty of the States, she entered into a close alliance with them, and sent an army **Leicester in** under the Earl of Leicester to their help, re- **Holland.** ceiving the towns of Brille and Flushing as security for her expenses (1585). In a skirmish between the English and Spaniards near Zutphen, Sir Philip Sidney, the accomplished author of *Arcadia* and the ideal embodiment of English chivalry, fell (1586). Leicester was unable to cope with Parma, and was recalled. In other quarters, however, more injury was inflicted on the Spaniards. Philip had seized all English ships and seamen in Spanish harbours, and in revenge for this Drake had been sent on a fresh expedition. Sailing across to the West Indies, he stormed and plundered San Domingo and other settlements. Philip was filled with alarm and rage, and, urged on by Parma and the pope, at length resolved to undertake the conquest of England. For years Elizabeth and he had been indirectly striking at each other. On his side he had supported Mary's adherents in England and abroad, encouraged the Jesuits and seminary priests, and harassed the English queen in Ireland, while she on her side had aided the Netherlanders and let loose Drake and the "sea-dogs" against Spanish colonies and ships. They now stood face to face as declared foes.

The pope had already given his sanction to the Queen's murder, and a fresh conspiracy was soon hatched. Babington and a number of Roman Catholic gentlemen, some of whom held offices in the royal household, entered into a scheme to kill Elizabeth. Their plot was detected by Walsingham, and Mary was found to be implicated in it (1586). Brought to trial before a special commission appointed under the statute of the preceding year, she was unanimously found guilty, but it was only after great hesitation that Elizabeth signed the warrant for her execution. Parliament boldly declared that "the queen's safety could no way be secured as long as the Queen of Scots lived". In February, 1587, Mary was beheaded at Fotheringay Castle in Northamptonshire. She was the "false Duessa" of Spenser's *Faerie Queene*. She had never given up her claim to be rightful Queen of England, and for eighteen years she had been the centre and soul of Roman Catholic intrigues and plots against "her dear sister" Elizabeth.

Babington's Plot.

Execution of Mary Stuart.

Mary's execution quickened the determination of Philip to invade England. She had bequeathed her claims on the English succession to him. He was thus no longer attacking England for the benefit of a princess who was half French by blood, but on his own behalf. The pope, Sixtus V., vehemently urged him forward, and agreed to contribute a large sum towards the "holy" undertaking. Elizabeth scarcely realised her danger. She was busily negotiating with Parma, and was ready to abandon the Dutch, if only Philip would respect their constitutional liberties and grant them such freedom of conscience as she herself allowed to Roman Catholics. In April, 1587, however, Drake was despatched to the coast of Spain. Running into Cadiz he burned the ships and stores which were being collected there for the invasion of England. His exploit, which he termed "singeing the King of Spain's beard", delayed the concentration of the Armada for a year. The time thus gained was valuable. The English fleet was equipped, and the main body of it stationed at Plymouth under the admiral, Howard of Effingham, to wait for the enemy's approach. *Drake at Cadiz.*

Towards the end of May, 1588, Philip's fleet, "the most fortunate and invincible Armada", as it was called, sailed from the Tagus with the benediction of the pope. It consisted of 132 ships, and had on board 22,000 soldiers, besides sailors, and 300 monks and officers of the Inquisition for the work of Romanising England. Its admiral, the Duke of Medina Sidonia, had orders to sail to Flanders and effect a junction with Parma, whose army of 17,000 veterans lay encamped around Dunkirk. By their combined forces the invasion of England was to be carried out. At the threatened attack the English national sentiment took fire. All classes rallied with enthusiasm in defence of their queen and country. Towns and private individuals fitted out ships to reinforce Elizabeth's navy of 34 vessels. The militia mustered in full strength, and in a few days an army of 17,000 men assembled at Tilbury under the command of Leicester to cover London. As the Armada moved slowly up the Channel, a running fight of six days took place. In this the advantage was all on the side of the English. Their superior speed and better manœuvring enabled them to cut off single ships and inflict heavy damage on the enemy. On July 27th Sidonia reached Calais and opened communications with Parma. The Flemish ports, *The Armada sails.*

however, were closely blockaded by Dutch and English ships, and his colleague was unable to move to join him. Driven in confusion from Calais harbour by a few fire-ships sent in by the English, the Armada was attacked off Gravelines on July 29th by the combined English fleet under Howard, Drake, and Hawkins. The English shot told with terrible effect on the Spanish galleons whose decks were crowded with soldiers. Sidonia's defeat was decisive, and he fled away northwards, the English pursuing him till they had neither ammunition nor food left. The spirit of the Spaniards was broken. No longer thinking of joining Parma, and shrinking from a fresh encounter with "those devils" the English, they essayed to return home round the north of Scotland. Winds and storms finished the work of the English guns; and only 53 shattered hulks of the "most fortunate and invincible Armada" ever made their way back to Spain.

Defeat of the Armada.

The "great enterprise" of Philip and the papacy had failed. England had repelled the attempt to fasten upon her neck the political yoke of Spain and the ecclesiastical yoke of Rome. She had shattered the tradition of Spanish invincibility, and vindicated her position as a first-class power. The onslaught of the Romanist reaction had been driven back, and the advantages won by the Reformation were now secure.

The victory was a national one. The secret of it lay in the strong patriotism and free spirit of the English people. Roman Catholics had worked with Protestants in the common cause. The English navy, too, though inferior in size, was superior in efficiency to the formidable Armada. Its ships, built under the eyes of Hawkins, could sail twice as fast, and their guns, although only half the number of the Spanish, were of heavier calibre and better served. Sidonia and the Castilian grandees were no match upon the sea for Howard and his lieutenants, Drake, Hawkins, Frobisher, and Winter. When the intended junction with Parma was prevented, the fate of the expedition was sealed.

England victorious.

CHAPTER IX.

CONCLUSION—ELIZABETH'S LATER YEARS (1588-1603)—THE TUDOR PERIOD.

While Elizabeth was engaged in meeting the attacks of Roman Catholicism and the Counter-Reformation, she had at the same time to struggle with tendencies of an opposite character. Her religious settlement had from the first failed to satisfy the advanced Protestants, who had fallen under the influence of Calvinistic teaching, and desired to carry out further reforms in the church. It was not long before they came into collision with the Queen. The first difference was caused by "the vestiarian controversy". The reformers, or "Puritans" as they became styled, objected to certain ceremonial observances, which appeared to them to savour of popery, such as the wearing of vestments, the making of the sign of the cross in baptism, and the use of the ring in marriage. For some time they were allowed to follow their own course: the rubrics were not complied with; great varieties in ceremonial between different places were the result. At last, in 1566, Elizabeth, whose own tastes were in favour of elaborate ritual and outward show, caused Archbishop Parker to issue his *Advertisements*, enjoining the use of the surplice and certain other observances on all clergymen under pain of dismissal. Most of the objectors gave way, but in the diocese of London thirty-seven proved recalcitrant and were deprived of their cures. As the struggle with Rome deepened English Protestantism inevitably became sterner and more anti-papal in character; Puritanism increased, and found powerful supporters both at court and in Parliament. In 1571 bills were introduced in the Commons for amending the Prayer-book so as to meet the scruples of the reformers, but on the personal intervention of the Queen they were dropped.

The early Puritans.

Meanwhile Puritanism had entered upon a new phase.

No longer confining itself to ceremonial points, it proceeded to attack the established form of church government, condemning episcopacy and aiming at replacing it by the rule of presbyters and elders according to the model instituted by Calvin. The most prominent advocate of these views was Thomas Cartwright, a Cambridge professor of divinity, who had studied at Geneva. He was mainly responsible for the *Admonitions to Parliament* (1572), and the *Book of Discipline*, in which the Presbyterian system was expounded. That system, if logically applied, would have brought in an ecclesiastical despotism. It gave to the church and its officers an absolute supremacy over the state. It made the minister or preacher omnipotent in his own congregation, investing him with power to excommunicate offenders and to call in the civil authority to his support. It thus cut at the essential principle of the English Reformation, which had been the subordination of the church to the state and the subjection of the clergy to the secular courts. Many of the former abuses would have returned in a fresh shape. As Milton saw, "New Presbyter was but old Priest writ large".

The teaching of Cartwright and his friends, although it took little root among the people at large, met with considerable favour among the clergy, whose principal text-book of theology was now Calvin's *Institutes*. About this time, too, "exercises" or "prophesyings" came into fashion in many places. These were meetings for the discussion of religious and ecclesiastical subjects, and naturally afforded great opportunities for calling attention to evils in the church and disseminating Puritan ideas. In Sussex and the Midland Counties steps were taken towards introducing the Presbyterian system indirectly by the formation of voluntary associations or "classes" of clergy. The Queen viewed the Presbyterian movement with dislike. She saw its revolutionary and democratic tendencies. It threatened her supremacy, which was exercised through the agency of the bishops, and was disturbing the unity of the church in the very face of the Romanist attacks.

The Presbyterian movement.

She set herself against it. Grindal, who had succeeded Parker in the see of Canterbury, and who was half a Puritan himself, declined to put down the prophesyings at her behest, perceiving their value in training preachers and stimulating their zeal. He was in consequence suspended from his see for five years. His successor, Whitgift, who became primate in 1583, was a man after Elizabeth's own heart. "Those vain prophesyings" were at once suppressed. A stricter uniformity was insisted on. The High Commission Court, which Elizabeth had established for enforcing the Acts of Supremacy and Uniformity, became a far more active and efficient instrument in the hands of Whitgift. Its energies were now directed mainly against the Puritans. Its powers were extensive. It could inflict almost any penalty except death and torture. It could, by means of the "ex-officio oath", compel the accused to answer questions put to him and thus give evidence against himself. Twenty-four stringent interrogatories were now drawn up by Whitgift and administered to clergymen suspected of unorthodoxy. Many who had Presbyterian leanings were deprived of their benefices. The archbishop's proceedings evoked many protests, Burghley himself declaring that they "savoured of the Romish Inquisition, and were rather a device to seek for offenders than to reform any". *The High Commission Court.*

Elizabeth's action against the Puritans was partly prompted by the appearance of doctrines among them, which were still more subversive of her ecclesiastical supremacy and of the organisation of the national church. Shortly after 1580 the Brownists or Separatists came into existence, and in the ensuing years their tenets spread rapidly. The ancestors of the Independents, they held that each congregation was a complete and independent church in itself. They were the first Dissenters. Unlike the older Puritans, who remained within the fold of the church and strove to reform its regulations and government according to their ideas, the Brownists held aloof from the church and claimed the *The Brownists.*

right to organise themselves in complete separation from it. Goaded by persecution, their attacks on episcopacy grew more and more vehement. Their influence was seen in the *Martin Mar-prelate Tracts*, which were published about 1588, and were full of the most scurrilous invective against the bishops and clergy. The archbishop was described as "the Canterbury Caiaphas, a monstrous Anti-Christ"; the bishops as "incarnate devils, cozening knaves, enemies of God"; the clergy as "dolts, hogs, drunkards, desperate and forlorn atheists". By such virulent abuse the Brownists defeated their own object and alienated sympathy from themselves. It was against them that the statute of 1593, the first enactment of the reign against Protestant sectaries, was levelled. It punished frequenters of conventicles with imprisonment, and, if they still refused to conform, with banishment and even death. Many of the Brownists fled from the country "for conscience sake" and settled in Holland. Some of these exiles in later years sailed in the *Mayflower* to seek a new home in America (1620).

Elizabeth had thus been led by circumstances to forsake her tolerant policy and to persecute both Puritan and Roman Catholic dissentients. Puritanism, however, unlike Roman Catholicism, had never been tainted with treason: it was fervently loyal to her. The penal statutes against Romanism continued to be put in force after the defeat of the Armada. They were completed in 1593 by an act which forbade "popish recusants" to travel more than five miles from their homes, and ordered all who broke its provisions and were unable to pay the recusancy fines to abjure the realm. The concluding years of Elizabeth's reign were years of religious quiet. The bulk of the nation had rallied round her religious settlement. The Roman Catholics had been reduced to a small and well-nigh harmless sect. The High Commission Court had crushed the Presbyterian movement among the clergy. Moreover, in 1594, Richard Hooker had published the first four books of his *Ecclesiastical Polity*, which was a temperate and learned defence of the arrangements of the national church against the attacks of Cartwright and the Puritans.

The discomfiture of the Armada had marked a decisive point in European history. It destroyed the belief that the military force of Spain was irresistible. The turn of the tide had come; and henceforth Spanish power gradually but surely declined. The English, who had been rendered confident by their victory, now became the attacking party, and proceeded to wreak a stern vengeance on Philip and his empire. A wave of crusading zeal against Spain and the Inquisition swept through the country. Spain instead of France became the national enemy. Year after year expeditions, fitted out chiefly at the expense of individuals, sailed forth to prey upon her commerce and plunder her towns and possessions. No part of her dominions was safe from their attacks. In the spring following the Armada (1589) a strong force under Norris and Drake was sent to the Peninsula to support the claims of Dom Antonio to the kingdom of Portugal, which Philip had annexed eight years before. A descent was made on the neck of land at the mouth of the Tagus, and the suburbs of Lisbon were seized. The Portuguese, however, did not rise in Antonio's favour, as had been expected; and although much injury was done to the enemy, the main object of the enterprise proved futile. The English commanders, having lost half their men by disease, returned home; their only successes had been the sack of the Spanish ports of Corunna on their way out, and Vigo on their way home. *The decline of Spain.* *The 'Journey of Portugal'.*

Philip's attention soon became centred on France, and the chief scene of the struggle between him and the English queen shifted to that country. In August, 1589, the French king, Henri III., was murdered by a Dominican friar, an emissary of the Catholics of the League. With him the Valois line came to an end. The nearest heir to the throne was the king of Navarre, who assumed the royal title as Henri IV. He was, however, a Huguenot in religion. The League, *Henri of Navarre.*

which was Roman Catholic rather than patriotic in feeling, and which now looked to Philip as its head, proclaimed the aged Cardinal of Bourbon, Henri's uncle, king, and recognised Philip as Protector of France in his behalf. The prospect of making France his dependency stirred the ambition of the Spanish monarch, and he set himself to crush Henri. He withdrew Parma and his army from the Netherlands to oppose him. Henri on his side received steady support from Elizabeth, who allied with him and sent him repeated supplies of men and money. The Cardinal soon died; and the Leaguers schemed to confer the French crown on the Infanta Isabella, daughter of Philip and grandchild of Henri II. A Spanish force invaded Brittany (1591), to which Isabella alleged a special claim as the descendant of the Duchess Anne. Elizabeth was alarmed. Norris was hurried across to keep the Spaniards in check; and shortly afterwards a fresh force was sent under Robert Devereux, Earl of Essex, to assist Henri in Normandy. Essex, who was only twenty-four years old, was a handsome and accomplished courtier, who had risen on Leicester's death (1588) to be the prime favourite of the Queen. Parma proved himself more than a match for the allied troops, and forced them to raise the siege of Rouen. His death in the following winter was an irreparable loss to Philip. The League, too, was losing ground. Its Spanish proclivities were arousing the French national sentiment against it. Henri, who took a politician's view of religion, saw his opportunity, and in July, 1593, was converted to the Roman Catholic faith. In a few months his authority was recognised in every part of France.

<small>Henri's conversion.</small>

Elizabeth still continued her support of Henri after his apostasy: their alliance was too firmly based on community of interest to be broken off. In 1596 the Spaniards invaded France and captured Calais. This success led Henri, Elizabeth, and the Dutch to draw together in a close league. The Queen was spurred into greater activity. A powerful armament was fitted out by the English and

Dutch, and sent under the command of the Lord Admiral, Howard of Effingham, and Essex to the coast of Spain. The harbour of Cadiz was forced and all the shipping in it burnt, while the town itself was taken by storm and pillaged (1596). *The sack of Cadiz.* This exploit was the severest blow that had yet been inflicted on the Most Catholic King. In the next year a fresh expedition, led by Essex and Sir Walter Raleigh, sailed to the Azores. Its two commanders, however, quarrelled, and failed to effect their object of intercepting the Spanish treasure-fleet. The capture of prizes was far more difficult than it had been. The Spaniards were everywhere upon the alert. There was "not a grain of gold, silver, or pearl but what must be got through the fire".

In the opening part of 1598 Henri concluded an advantageous peace with Philip at Vervins, thus deserting his allies, the English and Dutch. Shortly afterwards he issued the famous Edict of Nantes, by which he granted a wide measure of religious toleration to the Huguenots. In the autumn his enemy Philip sank into the grave, a broken and defeated man.

Meanwhile as the Queen grew old and her ministers died around her, her court became the scene of personal jealousies and intrigues for power. The long continuance of the war, too, led a peace-party to come into existence. Burghley himself, the uncompromising foe of Spain, believed that his great work had been done, and was inclined to listen to advantageous terms. But the younger men who had grown up during the struggle scorned his cautious policy, and were eager to prosecute the war with Spain to the bitter end. They caused the overtures for peace made by Philip at the time of the Treaty of Vervins to be rejected. Chief among them were Essex and Raleigh. In 1598 Burghley died. He *Death of Lord Burghley.* had served the Queen for forty years with unwavering faithfulness. His place as first minister passed to his son, Robert Cecil, whom he had carefully trained as his successor. Essex was deeply mortified. Generous towards his inferiors, he could not brook an equal, and hated

Cecil with all a rival's bitterness. Not content with the dignified position which Leicester had occupied by the side of the Queen, he burned to distinguish himself, and looked towards Ireland as a field for his ambition.

The severity with which the Desmond rising had been put down had for the time crushed all open resistance in Ireland. Perrot, too, who had been created Deputy in 1584, followed a conciliatory policy towards the native septs. It was not long, however, before the confiscation of MacMahon's lands re-awoke uneasiness in the north.

Unrest in Ireland. Papal and Spanish intrigues were also at work. Jesuits and seminarists flocked over and stirred up animosity against Elizabeth's ecclesiastical measures. The evil and effete condition of the reformed Irish Church heightened the effect of their preaching. Hostility to the Protestant worship, which the government essayed to enforce, gradually increased. The Anglican ritual was called the "devil's service", and the Irish crossed themselves at the sight of a Protestant.

The simmering discontent was taken advantage of by Hugh O'Neill, who had been brought up at the English court and created Earl of Tyrone. The nephew of **Essex and Tyrone.** Shane, it was his aim to recover all the predominance which his ancestors had formerly enjoyed in the island. His revolt was the most serious one that Elizabeth had had to meet. He procured arms and ammunition from Spain, and established his supremacy over the neighbouring chieftains. At Yellow Ford, near Armagh, he overthrew the English forces under Sir Henry Bagnal with great slaughter (1598). His victory was the signal for a general rising among the Irish. The English were everywhere attacked. Vigorous measures were seen to be necessary. The royal favourite, Essex, who had shown himself a gallant soldier at Cadiz and elsewhere, was at his own desire sent over as Lord-Lieutenant, and an army of 20,000 men was placed under his command (1599). Instead of attacking Tyrone at once, the Earl frittered away his strength in putting down the insurrectionary movements in the south. When at length he marched northwards, he admitted the archrebel to peace on terms which were absolutely impossible for the English government, and which lent colour to the suspicion that he was striving to create a powerful military position for himself. Complaints arose, and Essex, presuming on Elizabeth's favour, petulantly deserted his post in direct violation of her orders and hurried home. Such wilful disobedience deeply offended the Queen. "By God's son," she burst out, "I am no queen: this man is above me." The favourite was called to account and dismissed from his offices. His irritable temper could not endure his disgrace. He intrigued with the discontented Puritans and Roman Catholics, and urged James, the Scottish king, to exact by force the recognition of his claims to the English succession. Finally, with the help of a few confederates, he made a mad attempt to incite a rising in London against the government. He was in consequence executed as a traitor (February 1601). His insurrectionary effort, which had been largely prompted by jealousy of Cecil, showed a surviving trace of the hatred of the nobles for the "new men" whom the Tudors raised to ministerial power. *Essex's rebellion and death.*

Lord Mountjoy, who succeeded Essex in Ireland, found nearly the whole country under the sway of Tyrone. He pursued a policy of merciless severity towards the insurgents. In the autumn of 1601 a Spanish army landed on the south coast to assist the Irish, but Mountjoy blockaded it in Kinsale, and, completely defeating Tyrone when he marched to its relief, forced it to capitulate. Gradually the strength of the rebels was worn down; and in 1603 Tyrone submitted, and, on renouncing Spain and his foreign allies, was pardoned.

On March 24th, 1603, the Queen died. She was the last of her line. She had been understood to indicate a wish that James of Scotland should succeed her. Vain, fitful, vacillating, Elizabeth nevertheless possessed all the Tudor capacity for ruling. Under her England had risen to a commanding position *Character of Elizabeth.*

in Europe. Her diplomacy, in spite of its apparent capriciousness, had yet had the solid merit of success. The taxation had been light, and the internal prosperity of the country had progressed by leaps and bounds. Her help, often dealt out with a niggardly hand, had enabled the Dutch and Henri to resist the aggressions of Philip. The independence of the United Provinces, which Spain virtually acknowledged in 1609, was largely her work. She won, as no sovereign had won before her, the love and affection of her subjects, "her many husbands", as she called them, and succeeding generations looked back with patriotic pride to the reign of the great queen, "of famous memory".

With the death of Elizabeth the Tudor epoch came to a close. It had seen the establishment of a strong centralised power in England. The crown had shaken off the weakness which had characterised it in the preceding period and had become practically absolute. It had won supremacy over the church in addition to supremacy over the state. The Tudor rule was arbitrary and autocratic in character. It was exercised in and by means of the Council, or Privy Council, as it was otherwise called. The Tudor government was "a government by council". But the Council, being nominated by the monarch, was merely his instrument: "it willed what he willed". It was entirely dependent upon him, and never dreamt of opposing his wishes. Its powers were immense. It could, by issuing proclamations, supplement and expand the law. It superintended the whole administration. The executive or governmental machinery, which was greatly enlarged during the Tudor reigns, was centred in it. It also constituted when sitting in the Star Chamber the most important tribunal of the realm. The Star Chamber Court was merely the Privy Council acting in its judicial capacity. The sphere of action of that court was unlimited. It could interfere in all matters, whether small or great. In violation of the common law of England it employed torture as a means of procuring

The Tudor regime.

The Council under the Tudors.

evidence. It could impose any penalty short of death. Its arm could reach the mightiest. It watched over judges, juries, and justices of the peace, and made them do their duty. Above all, it put down the turbulence of the nobles, "bridling such stout noblemen or gentlemen which would offer wrong by force to any meaner men". It was the principal security for order in this period. Its unpopularity arose only under the Stuarts. It enforced the royal power over the state, just as the High Commission Court enforced the royal power over the church.

The Tudor rule, however, was not a tyranny. It did not rest, like the French monarchy, on the possession of a standing army and the power of arbitrary taxation. The Tudor sovereigns possessed neither the one nor the other. Their rule was rather a *dictatorship*. It was based on the assent of the nation, and it was assented to because in the main it identified itself with the national interests. The Tudors, unlike the Stuarts, were careful not to outrage popular opinion. Although they might not bend to it, still they were always anxious to bring it on their side. The National Assembly, the Parliament, still met, although less frequently than in the later Plantagenet era; but as against the king it had little independence. The Tudors acted through it, and used it as their agent: it was subservient to them. Various causes account for its subordinate position. The Civil War and the Tudor policy combined had broken the power of the great lords. The Commons were not yet strong enough to take the lead. They were, moreover, supporters of the royal authority, which encouraged them as a counterpoise to the nobles, and which suppressed baronial anarchy and gave them the security necessary for their trade. The monarch, too, had potent means of swaying and controlling the Houses. He could summon and dissolve Parliament at his will. He could influence elections, and so secure the return of members who favoured his views. The Speaker, the mouthpiece of the Commons and the controller of their debates, was his nominee. And he could extend the privilege of repre-

Parliament under the Tudors.

sentation as he chose, and confer it on boroughs where his own influence was predominant. In this way Elizabeth summoned sixty-two fresh members to the House.

The Tudors encouraged the parliamentary action of the Third Estate. Under them the Commons played a more important part than they had hitherto done. They thus grew stronger and more self-reliant, and were gradually fitted to throw off their tutelage to the crown. Even in the Tudor period their action at times showed signs of increasing independence on their part. Under Edward VI. they inserted, contrary to the Council's wishes, a clause in the new Treason Statute requiring the presence of at least two witnesses in trials of treason. They defeated Mary's plans of giving Philip a share in the government of the country, and restoring the confiscated monastic property to the church. In Elizabeth's reign they repeatedly interfered, in spite of the Queen's prohibition, in the questions of the royal succession and of the church. They stood up boldly in defence of their peculiar privileges. But their most notable victory was won in 1601 when, at their demand, the Queen withdrew "divers monopolies" or patents which she had granted, and which they condemned as abuses. As the Commons advanced in wealth and importance, the Tudor system would inevitably become more difficult to maintain.

Signs of Commons' growing independence.

There was during the period a wide extension of governmental action, and consequently of governmental machinery. A new system of local government was created. It was then that the parish, which had hitherto been an ecclesiastical area, and had existed merely for ecclesiastical purposes, was used and developed for civil business, —notably the relief of the poor and the repair of roads,—and made the unit of local administration. It superseded or absorbed the old township. Its officers, the rector and the churchwardens, whose duties so far had been purely religious, rose into important executive officials; and the church-meeting, the vestry, became the assembly for managing village affairs.

Local Government.

In the county the Tudors introduced a new officer, the lord-lieutenant, to preside over the militia and maintain order. But their most active agents in the shire were the Justices of the Peace, whose importance is entirely due to Tudor legislation. They gave the justices the right of preliminary inquiry in all criminal cases, and charged them with the duty of enforcing the police laws and superintending the parochial administration. In consequence of these arrangements the rural districts were far more efficiently governed than before. Local government continued much as the Tudors left it until the present generation.

The Tudor reigns, and in particular the reign of Elizabeth, were a time of great commercial development. Trade expanded in a manner altogether unprecedented. The prohibition against usury, or the taking of interest, was removed. Feudal labour disappeared, and was replaced by the free labour of modern times. Villainage died out. The inclosure-system, although causing hardship for the moment, represented a great economic advance, and enlarged the productive capacity of the land. The hop was introduced from the Netherlands, and the potato from America. English manufactures increased. The woollen industry was stimulated by the arrival of Flemish refugees, who brought in the weaving of finer sorts of cloth. There was a vast mass of legislation upon commercial subjects. In 1566 Gresham founded the Royal Exchange. Trade was opened out with fresh districts, companies being formed for the purpose, and receiving charters from the crown. The Turkey Company was incorporated in 1581, and the famous East India Company in 1600. It was a time of great maritime adventure. Voyages of discovery were made to the Arctic regions, the South Pacific, and the East Indian Seas. English colonisation began. Raleigh, in 1584, founded the colony of Virginia in America, and Frobisher, in attempting to find a north-west passage to India, took possession of a large area round Hudson's Bay in the name of the English queen.

Commerce.

Side by side with this commercial development there was much misery among certain sections of the population. The extinction of villainage and break-up of the manorial organisation, the spread of "inclosures" and the dissolution of the great households of the nobles by the Star Chamber, had alike cast numbers adrift without employment and without means of support. Vagrants abounded. It was this state of affairs that led the government to concert measures for the relief of the indigent. At first a voluntary method was tried, an act of 1535 ordering collections to be made on Sundays in the churches. This, however, proved insufficient, especially when the monasteries came to an end. "Kind persuasion" was gradually replaced by compulsion. Finally the system of poor-relief was settled by the statute of 1601, which created new parochial officers, "overseers of the poor", to administer relief to the poor of the parish, and empowered them to levy a rate for the purpose. This act forms the basis of the modern poor-laws.

<small>The Poor Law.</small>

Moreover, in the Tudor period, a rich national literature was born. The barrenness which had marked the fifteenth century disappeared, and from 1550 onwards there came an outburst of literature which has never been equalled in any country. It was the English Renaissance. Modern English came into being. The diction used is no longer that of Caedmon or even Chaucer, but such as is easily understood by the ordinary modern reader. In all departments of literature the era was a great one. It saw alike the birth of English prose, the origin of the national drama, and the elaboration of poesie. Latin had hitherto been the literary language. It was Ascham, the author of *The Schoolmaster*, who first set himself, as he says, "to write English matters in the English tongue for Englishmen". His example was followed by Lyly in *Euphues*, and by Sir Philip Sidney in *Arcadia*. The masterpiece of Elizabethan prose was Hooker's *Ecclesiastical Polity*. Pamphlets, too, were written in the vulgar tongue, and issued broad-

<small>Elizabethan Literature.</small>

cast by the printing-press, the most remarkable instances being the *Mar-prelate Tracts*. But famous as Elizabeth's reign is for the rise of English prose, it is still more famous for the origin and swift growth of the national drama. The first efforts of English play-writing were cramped by slavish adherence to classical models; but Marlowe, the author of *Doctor Faustus* and *The Jew of Malta*, liberated it from its fetters and gave it freedom of expression, developing, or indeed inventing, blank verse as its instrument. In the hands of Shakspere it reached a height of perfection which has never been surpassed. The greatness of that prince of dramatists lies in the fact that he is so "pre-eminently natural". Ben Jonson, who about 1594 wrote *Every Man in his Humour*, belongs mainly to the Jacobean epoch. In poesie, too, there was a rich harvest. New forms of poetical composition appeared. The sonnet, introduced from Italy by the Earl of Surrey and Wyatt, was cultivated to an extraordinary degree, notably by Spenser and Sidney. Poetical writing of all kinds abounded, from the lengthiest of allegories to the briefest of songs. The primacy among the Elizabethan bards belongs to Spenser, whose great work was *The Faerie Queene*. English historical writing, too, began with Holinshed's *Chronicles*, while Francis Bacon created a new species of prose composition in his *Essays* (1597).

The Tudor rule had done much for the greatness of the country. Wales was finally incorporated with England by Henry VIII., and given the right of sending representatives to the English Parliament. The same monarch raised Ireland to the rank of a kingdom; and at the death of Elizabeth, Scotland became joined to this country. The United Kingdom was thus complete. A powerful executive was developed, without which, as the Lancastrian reigns had shown, constitutionalism is only another name for oppression and anarchy. Internal order was established. The English navy, which had been virtually created by Henry VIII., was now, after the repulse of the Armada, mistress of the seas. And England, compact and secure at home, was entering upon her imperial career and preparing to build up an empire in America in the West and India in the East.

The era was a great era of transition. It saw mediævalism pass away and a new régime arise. It saw the church reformed, the administration reorganised, the social system transformed. It saw the growth of a great national literature, and the first beginnings of a worldwide commerce. It was the time when modern England was born.

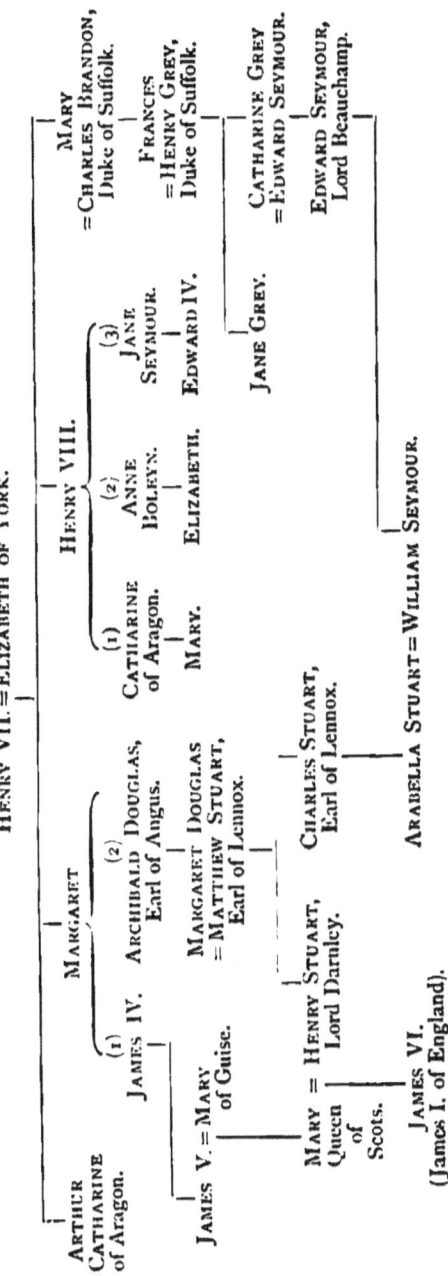

INDEX.

Adrian VI., Pope, 38.
Agriculture. new methods of, 74.
Albany, John, Duke of, regent of Scotland, 32, 35.
Alençon, Duke of, suitor of Elizabeth, 115; regent of the Netherlands, 116.
Alexander VI., Pope, 42.
Alva, Duke of, his cruelty in the Netherlands, 103; his victories, 109, 110.
America, discoveries of Cabot and Columbus in, 26; voyages of Drake to, 111, 117; English settlement in, 133.
Ancrum Muir, battle of, 68.
Angus, Archibald Douglas, Earl of, marries Queen Margaret, 32.
Anjou, Henri, Duke of, suitor of Elizabeth. *See* Henri III.
Annates Bill, the, 52.
Anne, Duchess of Brittany, her troubles, 14.
Anne Boleyn, marries Henry VIII., 53; divorced and executed, 57.
Anne of Cleves, married to and divorced from Henry VIII., 65, 66.
Armada, the Spanish, 119, 120.
Arran, Earl of, regent of Scotland, 68; suitor of Elizabeth, 91.
Arthur, Prince of Wales, son of Henry VII., marriage and death of, 19, 23.
Articles, the Six, 64, 65, 66; repealed, 73; the Forty-two, 78; the Thirty-nine, 90.
Ascham, Roger, his works, 134.
Aske, Robert, leader of the Pilgrimage of Grace, 61.
Askew, Anne, burnt, 66.

Babington, Anthony, his plot against Elizabeth, 118.
Bartholomew, St., massacre of, 109.
Barton, Elizabeth, the Nun of Kent, 54, 55.
Beaton, David, Cardinal, 67; his murder, 69.
Benevolences, raised by Henry VII., 22.
Bible, the, translated into English, 49, 58.

Blackheath, battle of, 18.
Bloody Statute, the, 66.
Bond of Association, the, 117.
Bonner, Edmund, Bishop of London, persecutes Protestants, 86.
Bothwell, James Hepburn, Earl of, murders Darnley, 95; marries Mary, Queen of Scots, 96.
Boulogne, capture of, 68; surrendered to Henri II., 77.
Brittany, wars in, 13.
Brownists, the, 123.
Buckingham, Edward Stafford, Duke of, executed, 36.
Burleigh, Robert Cecil, Lord, minister of Elizabeth, 88, 105; dies, 127.

Cabot, John and Sebastian, voyages of, 26.
Cadiz, Drake's expedition to, 119; taken by Essex, 127.
Calais, lost by Queen Mary, 87.
Calvinism, spread of, in England, 106.
Cambrai, league of, 28; peace of, 41.
Campeggio, Cardinal, papal legate, 41.
Campion, Edmund, Jesuit, executed, 115.
Cartwright, Thomas, Puritan divine, 122.
Casket Letters, the, 103.
Catharine of Aragon, married to Prince Arthur, 19; to Henry VIII., 23; divorced by him, 40–53.
Catharine Howard, married to and executed by Henry VIII., 66.
Catharine Parr, last wife of Henry VIII., 66.
Cecil, Robert, the elder, *see* Burleigh.
Cecil, Robert, the younger, minister of Elizabeth, 127.
Charles, Archduke of Austria, suitor of Elizabeth, 91.
Charles V., emperor, 33; allied to Henry VIII., 34; his wars with France, 34; selfish policy of, 35, 38.
Charles VIII. of France, his wars with Henry VII., 13–15.
Charles IX. of France, orders massacre of St. Bartholomew, 109.

Clement VII., Pope, his action on Henry VIII.'s divorce, 40-54.
Colet, Dean, 45, 46.
Columbus, Christopher, discovers America, 26.
Commerce under the Tudors, 133.
Congé d'élire, institution of, 54.
Convocation, submits to Henry VIII., 51.
Counter-Reformation, the, 111, 112.
Coverdale, Roger, 49; his translation of the Bible, 58.
Cranmer, Thomas, archbishop of Canterbury, 53; counsels Henry VIII.'s divorce, 50, 53; compiles the Prayerbook, 78; deposed and burnt by Mary, 82, 86.
Cromwell, Thomas, Earl of Essex, his rise to power, 52; policy of, 58; disgraced and executed, 65, 66.

Darnley, Henry, Lord, marries Mary, Queen of Scots, 94; murdered, 95.
Desmond, Garrett, Earl of, rebellion of, 113, 114.
Devon, Edward Courtenay, Earl of, released from the Tower, 81; conspires against Mary, 83.
Devonshire, rebellions in, 76.
Drake, Sir Francis, circumnavigates the world, 111; expedition to Cadiz, 119; to West Indies, 117.
Dudley, Edmund, minister of Henry VII., 23; beheaded, 28.
Dudley, Guilford, Lord, marries Lady Jane Grey, 79; beheaded, 84.
Dudley, John, Lord, Earl of Warwick, *see* Northumberland.
Dudley, Robert, Earl of Leicester, suitor of Elizabeth, 91.

Ecclesiastical courts, powers of, 44; restricted, 51.
Edward VI., birth of, 64; accession of, 71; reign of, 71-79; dies, 80.
Elizabeth, Queen, birth of, 57; accession of, 88; religious policy of, 89; her troubles with Mary of Scotland, 91-96, 116-118; her foreign policy, 91, 92, 93; her prosperous rule, 96; excommunicated by Pius V., 105; war with Spain, 119; later years of, 123-130; dies, 130.
Elizabeth of York, marries Henry VII., 11; dies, 24.
Empson, Richard, minister of Henry VII., 23; beheaded, 28.
Erasmus, influence of, 45, 46.
Essex, Robert Devereux, Earl of, his expedition to Cadiz, 127; commands in Ireland, 128; his intrigues and execution, 129.

Etaples, peace of, 15.
Exeter, Henry Courtenay, Marquis of, beheaded by Henry VIII., 64.

Ferdinand of Aragon, allied to Henry VII., 14; tortuous policy of, 19, 25, 30.
Field of the Cloth of Gold, 34.
Fisher, Thomas, bishop of Rochester, 50; executed by Henry VIII., 56.
Fitzgerald, Lord Thomas, rebellion of, 55.
Flodden, battle of, 29, 30.
Francis I. of France, 32; at Field of Cloth of Gold, 34; wars of, with Henry VIII., 34, 35, 68, 69.
Francis II. of France, marries Mary, Queen of Scots, 73.
Frobisher, Martin, his voyages, 133.

Gardiner, Stephen, bishop of Winchester, 58; imprisoned by Somerset, 74; minister of Mary, 81, 85.
Gascoigne, chancellor of Oxford University, attacks the Papacy, 43, 60.
Geraldines, rebellion of the, 99.
Grey, Lady Jane, marries Guilford Dudley, 79; proclaimed queen, 80; executed, 84.
Grey, Lady Catherine, offends Elizabeth by her marriage, 95.
Grey, Lord Leonard, his victories in Ireland, 99, 100.
Grocyn, William, leader of the "New Learning", 45.
Guise, Henri, Duke of, his struggle with the Huguenots, 108.

Hawkins, Sir John, explorations of, 104; sent against the Spaniards, 110.
Henri II., king of France, his wars with England, 76.
Henri III. of France, assassinated, 125.
Henri IV., king of France, 125; aided by Elizabeth, 126; issued Edict of Nantes, 127.
Henry VII., his claim to the throne, 10; marries Elizabeth of York, 11; domestic policy of, 20, 21; his wars with France, 13; foreign policy of, 19, 23; effects of his reign, 20, 22, 23; dies, 26.
Henry VIII., married to Catharine of Aragon, 23; accession of, 27; his French and Scottish wars, 29-32; 34, 35; his foreign policy, 28; aspires to the Empire, 33; his divorce, 39-53; quarrels with the Papacy, 53; breach with Rome, 55; suppresses rebellions, 61, 62; dissolves the monasteries, 60, 62, 63; despotism of, 65; his later

INDEX.   141

religious policy, 65, 66; last wars with France and Scotland, 67, 68, 69; dies, 70.
Hertford, *see* Somerset.
High Commission, court of, 89, 123.
Holland rebels against Philip of Spain, 109; aided by Elizabeth, 117; aids Elizabeth against the Armada, 120.
Hooker, Richard, his *Ecclesiastical Polity*, 124.
Howard, Catharine, wife of Henry VIII., executed, 66.
Howard, of Effingham, Lord, defeats the Armada, 120.

India, first English trade to, 133.
Indulgences, Luther protests against, 48.
Intercursus Magnus, the, 17.
Ireland, rebellions in, against Henry VII., 15; rule of Poynings in, 17, 97; rebels against Henry VIII., 55; rebellions against Elizabeth in, 102; rebels under Desmond, 113, 114; under Tyrone, 128; subdued, 129; reformation in, 100, 101; Marian plantation in, 101.

James IV. of Scotland aids Perkin Warbeck, 17, 18; slain at Flodden, 29.
James V. of Scotland, his wars with Henry VIII., 67.
James VI. of Scotland, birth of, 95; intrigues at the court of, 112; dealings of, with Elizabeth, 112.
Jane Grey, Lady, her reign, 80; her execution, 84.
Jane Seymour, queen of Henry VIII., 57; dies, 64.
Jesuits, their intrigues against Elizabeth, 114; expelled from England, 117.
Jonson, Ben, his plays, 135.
Juan of Austria, son of Charles V., his victory at Lepanto, 108; governor of the Netherlands, 110; his projects against England, 111.
Julius II., Pope, instigates the League of Cambrai. 28; legalises marriage of Henry VIII., 40.
Justices of the Peace, their duties, 133.

Ket, Robert, rebellion of, 76.
Kildare, Gerald, Earl of, his rebellion, 99.
Kildare, Thomas, Earl of, Lord Deputy of Ireland, 97.
Kinsale, battle of, 129.

Latimer, Hugh, bishop of Worcester, his preaching, 74, 75; deposed, 82; martyred, 86.

Leicester, Robert Dudley, Earl of, favourite of Elizabeth, his expedition to Holland, 117; dies, 126.
Lennox, Esmè Stuart, Duke of, 112.
Lepanto, battle of, 108.
Linacre, Thomas, his work, 45.
Lincoln, John de la Pole, Earl of, rebels against Henry VII., 12.
Local Government under the Tudors, 132.
London, treaty of, 32.
Louis XII. of France, his wars with Henry VIII., 29; marries Mary of England, 31.
Lovell, Francis, Lord, rebels against Henry VII., 11, 12.
Luther, Martin, preaches against the Papacy, 48.

Maintenance, practice of, 8; statute against, 21.
Margaret Tudor, marries James IV. of Scotland, 19; marries Angus, 32.
Margaret, widow of Charles the Bold, aids Yorkish rebellions, 11, 12, 15.
Marignano, battle of, 32.
Marlowe, Christopher, his plays, 135.
Martin Mar-prelate Tracts, the, 124.
Mary, Queen of England, 80; crushes rebellion of Northumberland, 81, and of Wyatt, 84; marries Philip of Spain, 84; her persecutions, 85; war with France, 87; death, 87; her plantation in Ireland, 101.
Mary Tudor, daughter of Henry VII., marries Louis XII., 31; marries Charles Brandon, Duke of Suffolk, 32.
Mary of Guise marries James V. of Scotland, 67; regent of Scotland, 92.
Mary, Queen of Scots, birth of, 67; married to Francis II., 73; claims of to English crown, 91, 93; marries Darnley, 94; marries Bothwell, 96; forced to abdicate, 96; escapes to England, 96; tried by Elizabeth, 103; her conspiracies against Elizabeth, 116, 118; executed, 118.
Maximilian, Emperor, engages in the Breton War, 14; his negotiations with Henry VII., 14, 25; joins Henry VIII. in French war, 29.
Maynooth, capture of, 99.
Medina Sidonia, Duke of, commands the Armada, 119, 120.
Mercantile companies, rise of, 133.
Monasteries, corruption of the, 59; suppression of the lesser, 60; of the greater, 62, 63.
Moray, James, Earl of, 94; Regent of Scotland, 96; assassinated, 108.

INDEX

More, Sir Thomas, his works, 45, 46; Chancellor, 49; executed, 56.
Morton, Archbishop, 22.
Morton, Thomas Randolph, Earl of, regent of Scotland, 110; executed, 112.
Mountjoy, Lord, governor of Ireland, 129.

Netherlands, revolt of the, 108, 109.
Nonconformists, rise of the, under Elizabeth, 123, 124.
Norfolk, Thomas Howard, Duke of, imprisoned by Henry VIII., 70.
Norfolk, Thomas Howard, Duke of, conspires against Elizabeth, 105; executed, 107.
Northumberland, John Dudley, Duke of, suppresses Ket's rebellion, 76; made Protector, 77; policy of, 77, 78, 79; proclaims Lady Jane Grey, 80; executed, 81.
Northumberland, Thomas Percy, Earl of, heads rising in the north, 105.

Offaly, Lord, his rebellion, 99.
O'Neil, Shane, rebellion of, 102.
Orange, William I. of, heads Dutch insurgents, 109; assassinated, 116.
Oxford, John de Vere, Earl of, fined by Henry VII., 22.

Parker, Matthew, archbishop of Canterbury, 90; his ecclesiastical legislation, 121.
Parliament, Wolsey's dealings with, 37; the Reformation, 49–60; Elizabeth's dealings with, 131, 132.
Parma, Alexander Farnese, Duke of, governor in the Netherlands, 111; reconquers Belgium, 116.
Paul III., Pope, excommunicates Henry VIII., 57.
Pavia, battle of, 37.
Philip of Austria, archduke, his negotiations with Henry VII., 24.
Philip II. of Spain, married to Queen Mary, 84; proposes to marry Elizabeth, 91; his plots against Elizabeth, 107; sends out the Armada, 119; dies, 127.
Pilgrimage of Grace, the, 61.
Pinkie, battle of, 72.
Pius V., Pope, issues bull against Elizabeth, 105.
Pole, Henry Lord Montague, executed by Henry VIII., 64.
Pole, Reginald, his book on Unity, 59; Papal legate, 64, 83, 85; archbishop of Canterbury, 86; dies, 87.
Pole, de la, Henry and William, *see under* Lincoln and Suffolk, Earls of.

Poor Law, dealings of Elizabeth with, 134.
Portugal, conquered by Philip II., 115; English expedition to, 125.
Poynings' Acts, 97.
Præmunire, statute of, 43, 50, 85.
Prayer-book, 1st English, 73; 2nd, 78; reissued by Elizabeth, 89.
Privy Council, government of the, 130.
Prophesyings, the, 122.
Puritans, rise of the, 121.

Raleigh, Sir Walter, founds colony of Virginia, 133.
Recusancy Laws, the, 115.
Reformation, the, in Germany, 48; in England, 58, 59, 73; in Scotland, 92.
Renaissance, the, 45.
Ridley, Nicholas, bishop of London, martyred, 86.
Ridolfi Plot, the, 107.
Rising in the North, the, 105.
Rizzio, David, murder of, 95.
Rogers, John, martyred, 85.

St. Aubin, battle of, 14.
St. Bartholomew, massacre of, 109.
Scotland, *see under* James I. to VI., and Mary.
Seymour, Edward, Earl of Hertford, married to Catharine Grey, 95.
Seymour, Edmund, *see under* Somerset, Duke of.
Seymour, Jane, marries Henry VIII., 57; dies, 64.
Seymour, Thomas, Lord Sudeley, executed, 77.
Shakespeare, William, 135.
Sidney, Sir Henry, his successes in Ireland, 102.
Sidney, Sir Philip, slain at Zütphen, 117.
Simnel, Lambert, rebellion of, 12.
Sinclair, Oliver, commands Scottish army, 67.
Six Articles, the, 64, 65, 66; repealed, 73.
Skeffington, Lord-Deputy in Ireland, 99.
Smerwick, capture of, 114.
Solway Moss, battle of, 67.
Somerset, Edmund Seymour, Duke of, as Lord Hertford leads expedition against the Scots, 68; Protector of England, 71; his Protestantism, 73; his war with Scotland, 72; deposed, 77; executed, 78.
Spenser, Edmund, poet, his works, 135.
Spurs, battle of the, 29.
Stanley, Sir William, executed, 16.
Star-chamber, the, 130.
Stoke, battle of, 12.

INDEX.

Submission of the clergy, act of, 51, 53.
Suffolk, Charles Brandon, Duke of, marries Mary Tudor, 32; his commands in France, 35.
Suffolk, Henry de la Pole, Earl of, executed, 24.
Suffolk, Thomas Grey, Duke of, rebels against Mary, 83; executed, 84.
Supremacy, act of, 55, 56, 89.
Surrey, Henry, Earl of, executed, 70.
Surrey, Thomas, Earl of, wins battle of Flodden, 30.

Ten Articles, the, 58.
Terouane, siege of, 29.
Throgmorton, Francis, his plot, 116.
Tournay, siege of, 29.
Transubstantiation, doctrine of, 59.
Treason Bill, the, 78.
Trent, Council of, 69.
Tyndale, William, translates the Bible, 49.
Tyrone, Hugh O'Neil, Earl of, his rebellion, 128.

Uniformity, act of, 78, 79.
"Utopia", the, of More, 47, 74.

Virginia, colony of, founded by Raleigh, 133.

Wales incorporated with England by Henry VIII., 70, 135.
Walsingham, minister of Elizabeth, 118.
Warbeck, Perkin, his imposture, 15, 16, 18, 19.
Warwick, Edward Plantagenet, Earl of, imprisoned in the Tower, 12; executed, 19.
Warwick, John Dudley, Earl of, *see* Northumberland.
Westminster, see of, founded by Henry VIII., 63.
Westmoreland, Charles Neville, Earl of, his rebellion, 105.
Whitgift, John, archbishop of Canterbury, his dealings with Puritans, 123.
Wolsey, Thomas, minister of Henry VIII., 30; his foreign policy, 30-32, 39; his Church policy, 38, 48; his dealings with Henry's divorce, 39-41; his fall, 41; death, 42.
Wyatt, Sir Thomas, rebellion of, 83, 84.

Zütphen, battle of, 117.

PRINTED BY BLACKIE AND SON, LIMITED, GLASGOW.

BRIEF LIST
OF
EDUCATIONAL WORKS
PUBLISHED BY

BLACKIE & SON, LIMITED.

Classics.

CAESAR'S GALLIC WAR. Books I., II., III., IV., V., and VI. Edited, with Introduction, Notes, Exercises, and Vocabularies, by John Brown, B.A. With coloured Map, Illustrations, and Plans of Battles. F'cap 8vo, cloth, 1s. 6d. each.

CAESAR'S INVASIONS OF BRITAIN (Parts of Books IV. and V. of the Gallic War). Edited by John Brown, B.A. F'cap 8vo, cloth, 1s. 6d.

STORIES FROM CICERO. Edited, with Introduction, Notes, Exercises, and Vocabularies, by A. C. Liddell, M.A. F'cap 8vo, cloth, 1s. 6d.

HORACE'S HISTORICAL AND POLITICAL ODES. Edited, with Historical Introduction and Notes, by the Rev. A. J. Church, M.A. Crown 8vo, cloth, 2s. 6d.

STORIES FROM OVID. Edited, with Introduction, Notes, and Vocabulary, by A. H. Allcroft, M.A. Cloth, 1s. 6d.

VIRGIL'S AENEID. Book I. Edited, with Introduction, Outline of Prosody, Notes, Exercises on the Hexameter, Vocabulary, &c., by Rev. A. J. Church, M.A. F'cap 8vo, cloth, 1s.

THE STORY OF AENEAS: being Selections from the *Aeneid*, connected by a narrative in English. With Introduction, Notes, and Vocabulary, by A. H. Allcroft, M.A. With many illustrations. Part I. (Aeneid I.-VI.). F'cap 8vo, 2s.

SELECTIONS FROM PHAEDRUS, Books I. and II. Edited for Junior Forms, by S. E. Winbolt, B.A. Cloth, 1s.

CORNELIUS NEPOS: Select Biographies. Edited, with Introduction, Notes, Exercises, and Vocabularies, by J. E. Melhuish, M.A. F'cap 8vo, cloth, 1s. 6d.

A CLASSICAL COMPENDIUM: being a Handbook to Greek and Latin Constructions. By C. E. Brownrigg, M.A. 2s. 6d.

XENOPHON'S ANABASIS. Book I. Edited, with Introduction, Notes, an Appendix on Greek Constructions, and Vocabulary, by C. E. Brownrigg, M.A. With Map, Plans of Battles, &c. Cloth, 1s. 6d.

CORNELIUS NEPOS: SELECTIONS. Lysander, Alcibiades, Thrasybulus, Conon; Dion, Iphicrates, and Chabrias. Edited by A. W. Carver, M.A. Cloth, 1s.

LATIN STORIES: Short Selections from the best prose authors. Edited, with Notes, English Exercises, Vocabularies, &c., by A. D. Godley, M.A. 1s.

LATIN UNSEENS: Graduated Specimens of Prose and Verse, mainly selected from Examination Papers. *Junior Section*, 3d.; *Senior Section*, 6d.

LATIN PROSE OF THE SILVER AGE: SELECTIONS. Edited by C. E. Brownrigg, M.A. With an Introduction by T. H. Warren, M.A. 4s. 6d.

HINTS AND HELPS IN CONTINUOUS LATIN PROSE. By W. C. Flamstead Walters, M.A. F'cap 8vo, cloth, 2s. KEY, 2s. 6d. *nett*.

FIRST STEPS IN CONTINUOUS LATIN PROSE. By W. C. Flamstead Walters, M.A. Cloth, 2s.

HINTS AND HELPS IN CONTINUOUS GREEK PROSE. By W. C. Flamstead Walters, M.A. Cloth, 2s. 6d.

PRAXIS PRIMARIA: Exercises in Latin Composition. By the Rev. Islay Burns, M.A., D.D. Seventh Edition, crown 8vo, cloth limp, 2s. KEY, 3s. 6d.

GREEK UNSEENS, in Prose and Verse. Junior Section. Selected by A. C. Liddell, M.A. Paper cover, 4d.

MYTHS AND LEGENDS OF GREECE AND ROME. By E. M. Berens. Illustrated. F'cap 8vo, cloth, 2s. 6d.

English.

A SCHOOL HISTORY OF ENGLISH LITERATURE. By Elizabeth Lee. In four vols., f'cap 8vo, cloth, 1s. 6d. each.

Chaucer to Marlowe. *Now Ready.*
[Others to follow.

THE WARWICK LIBRARY. Comparative Manuals of English Literature. Crown 8vo, cloth, 3s. 6d. each. General Editor—Professor C. H. Herford, Litt.D.

English Pastorals. Edited by E. K. Chambers.
Literary Criticism. Edited by Professor C. E. Vaughan, M.A., University College, Cardiff.
English Essays. With an Introduction by J. H. Lobban, M.A., formerly Assistant Professor of English Literature in Aberdeen University.
English Lyric Poetry (1500-1700). With an Introduction by F. I. Carpenter, M.A., Ph.D.
[Others to follow.

The WARWICK SHAKESPEARE. The greater Plays, edited for students and senior candidates in the University Local Examinations. In f'cap 8vo, cloth.

As You Like It. Edited by J. C. Smith, M.A. 1s. 6d.
Twelfth Night. Edited by A. D. Innes, M.A. 1s. 6d.
Hamlet. Edited by E. K. Chambers, B.A. 1s. 6d.
Macbeth. Edited by E. K. Chambers, B.A. 1s.
Richard II. Edited by C. H. Herford, Litt.D., Professor of English at University College, Aberystwyth. 1s. 6d.
Julius Cæsar. Edited by A. D. Innes, M.A. 1s.
Henry the Fifth. Edited by G. C. Moore Smith, M.A. 1s. 6d.
Richard III. Edited by George Macdonald, M.A. 1s. 6d.
A Midsummer Night's Dream. Edited by E. K. Chambers, B.A. 1s. 6d.
The Tempest. Edited by F. S. Boas, M.A., sometime exhibitioner of Balliol College, Oxford. 1s. 6d.
Cymbeline. Edited by A. J. Wyatt, M.A. 1s. 6d.

Introduction to Shakespeare. By Professor Dowden. Illustrated. Cloth, 2s. 6d.

BLACKIE'S JUNIOR SCHOOL SHAKESPEARE. For junior candidates in the University Local Examinations, &c. Each f'cap 8vo, cloth.

Twelfth Night. Edited by Elizabeth Lee. 8d.
Hamlet. Edited by L. W. Lyde, M.A. 10d.
Macbeth. Edited by H. C. Notcutt, B.A. 8d.
King John. Edited by F. E. Webb, B.A. 8d.
The Merchant of Venice. Edited by George H. Ely, B.A. 8d.
Henry the Eighth. Edited by the same. 8d.
The Tempest. Edited by Elizabeth Lee. 8d.
Henry the Fifth. Edited by W. Barry, B.A.
Richard the Second. Edited by the same. 8d.
Coriolanus. Edited by Walter Dent. 10d.
Julius Cæsar. Edited by the same. 8d.
As You Like It. Edited by Lionel W. Lyde, M.A. 8d.
A Midsummer Night's Dream. Edited by W. F. Baugust, B.A. 8d.
Cymbeline. Edited by the same. 10d.

BLACKIE'S ENGLISH CLASSICS. Containing representative extracts from standard English authors, annotated for school use. Each f'cap 8vo, cloth.

ADDISON.—**Selected Essays.** Edited by the Rev. H. Evans, D.D. 2s.
ADDISON.—**Sir Roger de Coverley.** Edited by Frances E. Wilcroft. 1s.
BACON.—**Selected Essays.** Edited by the Rev. Henry Evans, D.D. 1s.
GOLDSMITH.—**She Stoops to Conquer** and **The Good-natured Man.** Edited by Harold Littledale, M.A. 1s.
MACAULAY.—**Horatius, Lake Regillus,** and **Prophecy of Capys.** 8d.
MILTON.—**Paradise Lost.** Edited by F. Gorse, M.A. Books I. II. and III., each 1s.
MILTON.—**Samson Agonistes.** Edited, with Introductions and Notes, by E. K. Chambers. 1s. 6d.
POPE.—**Essay on Criticism.** Edited by the Rev. Henry Evans, D.D. 1s.
SCOTT.—**The Lay of the Last Minstrel.** Complete, 1s.; Cantos I.-III., cloth, 9d.; Cantos IV.-VI., 9d.
SCOTT.—**The Lady of the Lake.** Edited by W. Keith Leask, M.A. 1s.

Readings from Carlyle. Edited by W. Keith Leask, M.A. Cloth, 2s. 6d.
The Citizen of the World. Select Letters. Edited by W. A. Brockington, M.A. Crown 8vo, cloth, 2s.
Essay on Addison. Edited by C. Sheldon, D.Litt. Crown 8vo, cloth, 2s.

JUNIOR SCHOOL CLASSICS. Each, with a few exceptions, 32 pages, with Biographical Sketch, Introductions, and Notes at end; paper, 2d.; cloth, 3d.

AYTOUN.—The Burial-March of Dundee.
BROWNING.—The Pied Piper of Hamelin. Edited by S. E. Winbolt, B.A.
BYRON.—The Prisoner of Chillon.
CAMPBELL.—Songs and Ballads. Edited by W. Dent.
OLD BALLAD.—Chevy Chase. Edited by S. E. Winbolt, B.A.
COLERIDGE.—The Rime of the Ancient Mariner. Edited by W. Dent.
COWPER.—John Gilpin, and other Poems. Edited by W. Dent.
GOLDSMITH.—The Deserted Village. Edited by Elizabeth Lee.

GOLDSMITH.—**The Traveller.** Edited by S. E. Winbolt, B.A.
GRAY.—**The Elegy, Eton College Ode, and The Bard.** Edited by Elizabeth Lee.
MACAULAY.—**Armada, Ivry, Battle of Naseby; Battle of Lake Regillus; Horatius.**
MACAULAY.—**Horatius and Battle of Lake Regillus,** in one volume, cloth, 6d.
MILTON.—**L'Allegro and Il Penseroso.** Edited by C. E. Browarigg, M.A.
SCOTT.—**Marmion.** Canto I., with Illustrated Notes, paper, 3d.; cloth, 4d. Canto II., paper, 2d.; cloth, 3d. Canto VI., 56 pp., paper, 3d.; cloth, 4d.
SCOTT.—**The Lay of the Last Minstrel.** Cantos I., II., III., IV., V., VI., each separately.
SCOTT.—**The Lady of the Lake.** Cantos I., II., III., IV., V., VI., each separately.
SHAKESPEARE.—**Selections from As You Like It. Selections from Julius Cæsar. Selections from The Merchant of Venice.**
WORDSWORTH.—**Selections from the Shorter Poems.** Edited by W. Dent.
BURNS.—**The Cotter's Saturday Night, &c.** *Notes below text.*
LONGFELLOW.—**Evangeline.** *Notes below text.* Paper, 3d.; cloth, 4d.

English Grammar, &c.

The PUPIL'S ENGLISH GRAMMAR: an Introduction to the study of English Grammar, based upon the Analysis of Sentences. F"cap 8vo, cloth, 1s. 6d.

HIGHER ENGLISH: a Course of English Study for Middle and Upper Forms. By David Campbell. F"cap 8vo, cloth, 1s. 6d.

LOWER ENGLISH: a Course of English Study for Lower Forms. By David Campbell. F"cap 8vo, cloth, 1s.

LESSONS ON ENGLISH FOR BEGINNERS. By David Campbell. Cloth boards, 1s.; limp cloth, 10d.

HANDBOOK OF ENGLISH COMPOSITION EXERCISES. Short Stories, Subjects, and Hints for Essays, Rules and Models for Letters, &c. F"cap 8vo, cloth, 1s.

STORIES AND ESSAYS. Carefully arranged and graduated Stories for Exercises, with classified Examples for Essays. F"cap 8vo, cloth, 1s.

SELECTIONS FOR PARAPHRASING. Selected by W. Murison, M.A. Cloth, 1s.

BAYNHAM'S ELOCUTION: Selections from leading Authors and Dramatists. By George W. Baynham. Crown 8vo, cloth, 2s. 6d.

THE PRACTICAL ELOCUTIONIST. By John Forsyth. Crown 8vo, cloth, 2s. 6d.

Modern Languages.

MODERN FRENCH TEXTS. Edited by Francis Storr, B.A. F"cap 8vo, 1s.
Lettres de Paul-Louis Courier. Edited by J. G. Anderson, B.A. Lond., prizeman in French. Cloth, 1s.
The Court of Spain under Charles II., and other Historical Essays by Paul de Saint-Victor. Edited by Francis Storr. Cloth, 1s.
Voyages en Zigzag. By Rodolphe Töpffer. Edited by Ascott R. Hope. 1s.
The Siege of Paris. By Francisque Sarcey. Edited by F. B. Kirkman. 1s.
Aimard's Les Trappeurs de L'Arkansas. Edited by Marguerite Ninet. Cloth, 1s.

A FIRST FRENCH COURSE. By J. J. Beuzemaker, B.A. Cloth, 1s. 6d.

A SECOND FRENCH COURSE. By J. J. Beuzemaker, B.A. Cloth, 2s. 6d.

FLEUR DE MER. By Pierre Maël. Edited by J. Boielle, B.ès-L. Cloth, 1s.

ACHILLE ET PATROCLE. Edited, with Notes, Exercises, &c., by Emile B. le François. Cloth, 8d.

FRENCH STORIES: a Reading-book for Junior and Middle Forms. With Notes, Exercises, &c. By Marguerite Ninet. 1s.

READINGS IN FRENCH. By Marguerite Ninet. F"cap 8vo, cloth, 1s. 6d.

FRENCH TALES FOR BEGINNERS. With complete Vocabularies. By Marguerite Ninet. Illustrated. Cloth, 1s.

A MODERN FRENCH READER: Interesting extracts from contemporary French. By J. J. Beuzemaker, B.A. Cloth, 1s.

FRENCH UNSEENS FOR JUNIOR FORMS. Passages in Prose and Verse. Selected by D. S. Rennard, B.A. 3d.

FRENCH UNSEENS FOR MIDDLE FORMS. Selected by E. Pellissier, M.A. F"cap 8vo, cloth, 1s.

FRENCH UNSEENS FOR UPPER FORMS. Selected by E. Pellissier, M.A. F"cap 8vo, cloth, 1s. 6d.

FRENCH IRREGULAR VERBS, fully conjugated, with Notes and Appendices. By Marcel Rosey. Paper, 6d.

HISTORICAL SKETCH OF FRENCH LITERATURE. By Marcel Rosey. 1s.

A COMPLETE COURSE OF FRENCH COMPOSITION AND IDIOMS. By Hector Rey, B.ès-L., B.Sc. Cloth, 3s. 6d.

A COMPREHENSIVE FRENCH MANUAL. For Students Reading for Army and other Examinations. By Otto C. Näf, M.A. Lond. Crown 8vo, cloth, 3s. 6d.

A FIRST GERMAN COURSE. By A. R. Lechner. Crown 8vo, cloth, 1s. 6d.

A SECOND GERMAN COURSE. By H. Baumann, M.A. Crown 8vo, cloth, 2s. 6d.

GERMAN STORIES. With Notes, &c., by L. de Saumarez Brock. 1s. 6d.

GERMAN UNSEENS. Junior Section. Selected by D. S. Rennard, B.A. 4d.

SCHILLER'S SONG OF THE BELL, and other Poems. Edited by George Macdonald, M.A. Crown 8vo, cloth, 8d.

History.

THE OXFORD MANUALS OF ENGLISH HISTORY. Edited by C. W. C. Oman, M.A. In f'cap 8vo volumes, with maps, &c.; cloth, 1s.

I. **The Making of the English Nation**, B.C. 55—A.D. 1135. By C. G. Robertson, B.A.
II. **King and Baronage**, A.D. 1135-1328. By W. H. Hutton, B.D.
V. **King and Parliament**, A.D. 1603-1714. By G. H. Wakeling, M.A.
VI. **The Making of the British Empire**, A.D. 1714-1832. By Arthur Hassall, M.A.

A SUMMARY OF BRITISH HISTORY. With Appendices. By the Rev. Edgar Sanderson, M.A. Cloth, 1s.

A HISTORY OF THE BRITISH EMPIRE. By the Rev. Edgar Sanderson, M.A. 476 pp., cloth, 2s. 6d.

THE WARWICK ENGLISH HISTORY. A Sketch of the Development of England and the Empire. From B.C. 55 to the present time. Cloth, 3s. 6d.

THE WARWICK HISTORY READERS: Illustrated Reading Books in English History. Crown 8vo, cloth.

No. I. Simple Stories from English History. 8d.
No. II. Simple Stories from English History. 10d.
No. III. Stories from English History, B.C. 55—A.D. 1485. 1s.
No. IV. Stories from English History, 1485—1688. 1s. 4d.
No. V. Stories from English History, 1688 to Present Time. By J. H. Rose, M.A. 1s. 6d.
No. VI. History of England to 1603. By the Rev. Edgar Sanderson, M.A. 1s. 6d.
No. VII. History of England from 1603 to Present Time. By G. H. Ely, B.A. 1s. 9d.

AN EPITOME OF HISTORY, Ancient, Mediæval, and Modern. By Carl Ploetz. Translated by W. H. Tillinghast. Crown 8vo, cloth, 7s. 6d.

THE SCOTS READER: a History of Scotland for Junior Pupils. By David Campbell. F'cap 8vo, cloth, 1s.

OUTLINES OF THE WORLD'S HISTORY, Ancient, Mediæval, and Modern. By Edgar Sanderson, M.A. Cloth, 6s. 6d.

Also:—Part I., ANCIENT ORIENTAL MONARCHIES, 1s.; Part II., GREECE AND ROME, 2s.; Part III., MEDIÆVAL HISTORY, 1s.; Part IV., MODERN HISTORY, 2s. 6d.

A SYNOPSIS OF ENGLISH HISTORY. By Herbert Wills. Crown 8vo, cloth, 2s.

A SYNOPSIS OF SCOTTISH HISTORY. By Herbert Wills. Crown 8vo, cloth, 2s.

OUR COUNTRY: a History for Lower Forms. By the Rev. Edgar Sanderson, M.A. Illustrated. Cloth, 1s. 4d.

THE STORY OF ENGLAND: a History for Lower Forms. By the Rev. Edgar Sanderson, M.A. Illustrated. Crown 8vo, cloth, 1s. 6d.

The two volumes "Our Country" and "The Story of England" are complementary of each other. Each traverses the field of English History, but the first deals at greater length with the early history, and touches more fully upon the romantic episodes than the other.

Geography.

MAN ON THE EARTH: a Course in Geography. By Lionel W. Lyde, M.A. Fully illustrated. Crown 8vo, cloth, 2s.

BLACKIE'S DESCRIPTIVE GEOGRAPHICAL MANUALS. By W. G. Baker, M.A.

No. 1. Realistic Elementary Geography. Taught by Picture and Plan. 1s. 6d.
No. 2. The British Isles. 2s.
No. 3. The British Colonies and India. 2s.
No. 4. Europe (except the British Isles). Crown 8vo, cloth, 2s.
No. 5. The World (except the British Possessions). Crown 8vo, cloth, 2s.

THE GEOGRAPHY OF THE BRITISH EMPIRE. By W. G. Baker, M.A. Cloth, 3s. 6d.

ZEHDEN'S COMMERCIAL GEOGRAPHY OF THE WORLD. Translated from the German of Professor Zehden, Handelsakademie, Leipzig. Second Edition, corrected to date, 592 pages, crown 8vo, cloth, 5s.

AUSTRALASIA: a Descriptive Account of the Australian and New Zealand Colonies. By W. Wilkins. Illustrated. Crown 8vo, cloth, 2s. 6d.

A PRONOUNCING VOCABULARY OF MODERN GEOGRAPHICAL NAMES. By George G. Chisholm, M.A., B.Sc. F'cap 8vo, cloth, 1s. 6d.

A SYNOPTICAL GEOGRAPHY OF THE WORLD: a Concise Handbook for Examinations, and for general reference. With a complete series of Maps. Crown 8vo, cloth, 1s.

THE GEOGRAPHY OF NORTH AMERICA: a Synopsis with Sketch Maps. Cloth, 6d.

THE GEOGRAPHY OF ASIA: a Synopsis with Sketch Maps. Cloth, 6d.

THE CENTURY GEOGRAPHICAL HANDBOOKS: with Maps.

No. III. **England.** 16 pp., 2d.
No. IV. **British Isles.** 32 pp., 2d.
No. IV. A-B. **Scotland, Ireland, Canada, United States,** &c. 3d.
No. IV. c. **Europe, British North America, Australasia.** 48 pp., 3d.
No. V. **Europe.** 48 pp., 3d.
No. VI. **British Colonies and Dependencies.** Climate, Interchange of Productions. 3d.
No. VII. **United States.** Ocean Currents. 3d.
No. VII. B. **The World,** with exception of Europe. 4d.

Arithmetic.

LAYNG'S ARITHMETIC. By A. E. Layng, M.A. Part I. To Decimals and the Unitary Method. Crown 8vo, cloth, 2s. 6d., with or without Answers.

LAYNG'S ARITHMETICAL EXERCISES, for Junior and Middle Forms (5000 Exercises). Crown 8vo, 1s.; with Answers, 1s. 6d. Answers alone, 6d.

PICKERING'S MERCANTILE ARITHMETIC, for Commercial Classes. By E. T. Pickering. Cloth, 1s. 6d.

A COMPLETE ARITHMETIC. Cloth. With Answers, 1s. 6d. Exercises only, 192 pages, 1s. Answers alone, 6d.

EXAMINATION ARITHMETIC. Problems and Exercises (with Answers) from University Local Exam. Papers. By T. S. Harvey. Cloth, 2s. KEY, 4s. 6d.

Mathematics.

EUCLID'S ELEMENTS OF GEOMETRY. With Notes, Examples, and Exercises. Arranged by A. E. Layng, M.A. Books I. to VI., with XI., and Appendix. Crown 8vo, 3s. 6d.

BOOKS I. to IV. in one vol., 2s. 6d. BOOK I., 1s.; II., 6d.; III., 1s.; IV., 6d.; I.-II., 1s. 3d.; I.-III., 2s.; V. and VI. together, 1s.; XI., 1s. 6d.

KEY to BOOK I., 2s. 6d.; to Complete Euclid, 5s.

PRELIMINARY ALGEBRA. By R. Wyke Bayliss, B.A. 1s.

ALGEBRA. To Progressions and Scales of Notation. By J. G. Kerr, M.A. With Answers, f'cap 8vo, cloth, 2s. 6d.; without Answers, 2s.

ALGEBRAIC FACTORS. By Dr. W. T. Knight. F'cap 8vo, cloth, 2s. KEY, 3s. 6d.

ELEMENTARY TEXT-BOOK OF TRIGONOMETRY. By R. H. Pinkerton, B.A. F'cap 8vo, cloth, 2s.

MATHEMATICAL WRINKLES for Matriculation and other Exams. By Dr. W. T. Knight. F'cap 8vo, cloth, 2s. 6d.

AN INTRODUCTION TO THE DIFFERENTIAL AND INTEGRAL CALCULUS. With examples of applications to Mechanical Problems. By W. J. Millar, C.E. F'cap 8vo, cloth, 1s. 6d.

Science.

DESCHANEL'S NATURAL PHILOSOPHY. An Elementary Treatise. By Professor A. Privat Deschanel, of Paris. Translated and edited by Professor J. D. Everett, D.C.L., F.R.S. Medium 8vo, cloth, 18s.; also in Parts, limp cloth, 4s. 6d. each.

Part I.—**Mechanics, Hydrostatics,** &c.
Part II.—**Heat.**
Part III.—**Electricity and Magnetism.**
Part IV.—**Sound and Light.**

A TEXT-BOOK OF ORGANIC CHEMISTRY. By A. Bernthsen, Ph.D. formerly Professor of Chemistry in the University of Heidelberg. Translated by George M'Gowan, Ph.D. Crown 8vo, cloth, 7s. 6d.

FUEL AND REFRACTORY MATERIALS. By A. Humboldt Sexton, F.I.C., F.C.S., Professor of Metallurgy in the Glasgow and West of Scotland Technical College. Crown 8vo, cloth, 5s.

A TEXT-BOOK OF SOLID OR DESCRIPTIVE GEOMETRY. By Alex. B. Dobbie, B.Sc. Crown 8vo, cloth, 2s.

HEAT AND THE PRINCIPLES OF THERMO-DYNAMICS. By C. H. Draper, D.Sc., B.A. Cloth, 4s. 6d.

HYDROSTATICS AND PNEUMATICS. By R. H. Pinkerton, B.A. Cloth, 4s. 6d.

AN ELEMENTARY TEXT-BOOK OF ANATOMY. By Henry Edward Clark, M.B.C.M., Professor of Surgery in St. Mungo's College, Glasgow, &c., &c. Crown 8vo, cloth, 5s.

ELEMENTARY PHYSIOLOGY. By Prof. Ainsworth Davis, Examiner in Botany, Physiology, and Hygiene to the Intermediate Schools of Wales and Monmouthshire. Cloth, 2s.

THE STUDENT'S INTRODUCTORY TEXT-BOOK OF SYSTEMATIC BOTANY. By Joseph W. Oliver. Illustrated. Cloth, 4s. 6d.

ELEMENTARY TEXT-BOOK OF PHYSICS. By Professor Everett. F'cap 8vo, cloth, 3s. 6d.

OUTLINES OF NATURAL PHILOSOPHY. By Professor J. D. Everett. F'cap 8vo, cloth, 4s.

THEORETICAL MECHANICS. By R. H. Pinkerton, B.A. F'cap 8vo, cloth, 2s.

ELEMENTARY TEXT-BOOK OF DYNAMICS AND HYDROSTATICS. By R. H. Pinkerton, B.A. F'cap 8vo, cloth, 3s. 6d.

THE ARITHMETIC OF MAGNETISM AND ELECTRICITY. By Robert Gunn. F'cap 8vo, cloth, 2s. 6d.

MAGNETISM AND ELECTRICITY. By W. Jerome Harrison and Charles A. White. F'cap 8vo, cloth, 2s.

LIGHT, HEAT, AND SOUND. By Charles H. Draper, D.Sc. (Lond.). F'cap 8vo, cloth, 2s.

ELEMENTARY INORGANIC CHEMISTRY: Theoretical and Practical. By Professor A. Humboldt Sexton. F'cap 8vo, cloth, 2s. 6d.

CHEMISTRY FOR ALL, or Elementary Alternative Chemistry in accordance with the Science and Art Syllabus. By W. Jerome Harrison, F.G.S., & R. J. Bailey. F'cap 8vo, 1s. 6d.

QUALITATIVE CHEMICAL ANALYSIS, Inorganic and Organic. By Edgar E. Horwill, F.C.S. F'cap 8vo, cloth, 2s.

AN ELEMENTARY TEXT-BOOK OF PHYSIOLOGY. By J. M'Gregor-Robertson, M.A., M.B. F'cap 8vo, cloth, 4s.

ELEMENTARY PHYSIOLOGY. By Vincent T. Murché. F'cap 8vo, cloth, 2s.

ELEMENTARY BOTANY. By Joseph W. Oliver. F'cap 8vo, cloth, 2s.

AN ELEMENTARY TEXT-BOOK OF GEOLOGY. By W. Jerome Harrison, F.G.S. F'cap 8vo, cloth, 2s.

AN ELEMENTARY TEXT-BOOK OF APPLIED MECHANICS. By David Allan Low. F'cap 8vo, cloth, 2s.

EARTH-KNOWLEDGE. PART 1. A Text-book of Elementary Physiography. By W. Jerome Harrison, and H. Rowland Wakefield. F'cap 8vo, 2s.

ELEMENTARY AGRICULTURE. Edited by Professor R. P. Wright. F'cap 8vo, 1s. 6d.

ELEMENTARY HYGIENE. By H. Rowland Wakefield. F'cap 8vo, 2s.

ELEMENTARY HYGIENE. With an Introductory Section on Physiology By H. Rowland Wakefield. Cloth, 2s. 6d.

FOOD AND ITS FUNCTIONS. A Text-Book for Students of Cookery. By James Knight, M.A., B.Sc. Crown 8vo, cloth, 2s. 6d.

Science for Beginners.

CHEMISTRY FOR BEGINNERS. By W. Jerome Harrison. Cloth, 1s.

AGRICULTURE FOR BEGINNERS. Edited by Professor R. P. Wright. Cl., 1s.

BOTANY FOR BEGINNERS. By Vincent T. Murché. Cloth, 1s.

MAGNETISM AND ELECTRICITY FOR BEGINNERS. By W. G. Baker, M.A. Cloth, 1s.

MECHANICS FOR BEGINNERS. By David Clark. Cloth, 1s. 6d.

ANIMAL PHYSIOLOGY FOR BEGINNERS. With Coloured Illustrations. By Vincent T. Murché. Cloth, 1s. 6d.

SCIENCE READERS. Fully illustrated.

Natural History Course.

Country Stories: Infant Reader. 6d.
Book I.—Tales and Talks on Common Things Part I. 8d.
Book II.—Tales and Talks on Common Things. Part II. 10d.
Book III.—Seaside and Wayside; or, The Young Scientist. 1s.
Book IV.—Our Friends of the Farm. By the Rev. Theodore Wood. 1s. 4d.
Book V.—Animal and Plant Life. Part I. By the Rev. Theodore Wood. 1s. 6d.
Book VI.—Animal and Plant Life. Part II. By the Rev. Theodore Wood. 1s. 6d.

General Course.

No. IV. The Young Mechanics. 1s. 4d.
No. V. The Young Chemists. By W. Furneaux. Cloth, 1s. 6d.
No. VI.-VII. Lessons on Living. By H. Rowland Wakefield. Cloth, 1s. 6d.

Reading Books.

READINGS FROM STANDARD AUTHORS, &c. Each foolscap 8vo, strongly bound in cloth.

- The Spectator Reader: Selections from Addison's Spectator. 1s. 3d.
- Readings from Sir Walter Scott. 1s. 3d.
- Mary Queen of Scots: being Readings from THE ABBOT. 1s. 3d.
- Tales from Henty: being Selections from the Historical and other Romances of G. A. Henty. Illustrated. 1s. 6d.
- The Charles Dickens Reader. 1s. 4d.
- The Sovereign Reader, fully illustrated, forming a bright historical record of the events of Queen Victoria's Reign. By G. A. Henty. New Edition, brought up to date. 1s. 6d.
- The Citizen: HIS RIGHTS AND RESPONSIBILITIES. By Oscar Browning, M.A. 1s. 6d.
- The Newspaper Reader: Selections from the Journals of the Nineteenth Century. 1s. 6d.
- The British Biographical Reader. 1s. 6d.
- Readings from Robinson Crusoe. Illustrated by Gordon Browne. 1s. 3d.
- Blackie's Shakespeare Reader. 1s.

THE PALMERSTON READERS. New series of Reading Books *with Coloured Illustrations*. In Ten Books, including *The Sight and Sound Primers*.

Prospectus, with Specimen Pages, on application.

STORIES FOR THE SCHOOLROOM. Edited by J. H. Yoxall. Selections from the works of favourite modern authors, illustrated by leading artists. Five books, prices 8d. to 1s. 6d. Primers, 3d. to 6d.

THE CENTURY READERS. Six books, prices 8d. to 1s. 6d. Primers, 2½d. to 6d.

Drawing, Painting, Writing, &c.

VERE FOSTER'S DRAWING COPY-BOOKS. 72 Numbers at 2d. Complete Edition, in Eighteen Parts at 9d. (Each part complete in itself.)

VERE FOSTER'S MODEL DRAWING. Cloth, 1s. 6d.

VERE FOSTER'S RUDIMENTARY PERSPECTIVE. Cloth, 1s. 6d.

VERE FOSTER'S WATER-COLOUR DRAWING-BOOKS. With coloured facsimiles of original water-colour drawings, and hints and directions. *Complete List on application.*

POYNTER'S SOUTH KENSINGTON DRAWING-BOOKS. Issued under the direct superintendence of E. J. Poynter, P.R.A. *Complete List on application.*

A SELECTION FROM THE LIBER STUDIORUM OF J. M. W. TURNER, R.A. In Four Parts, square folio, 12s. 6d. each; or complete in Portfolio, £2, 12s. 6d.

VERE FOSTER'S WRITING COPY-BOOKS.

- Original Series, in Twenty-two Numbers, price 2d. each.
- Palmerston Series, in Eleven Numbers, on fine paper ruled in blue and red, 3d. each.
- Bold Writing, or Civil Service Series, in Twenty-seven Numbers, price 2d. each.
- Upright Series, in Twelve Numbers, 2d. each.

Dictionaries, &c.

The STUDENT'S ENGLISH DICTIONARY. By John Ogilvie, LL.D. *New Edition*, revised and enlarged by Charles Annandale, M.A., LL.D. Illustrated by 800 Engravings. Large f'cap 4to, cloth, 7s. 6d.; half-persian, 10s. 6d.; half-morocco, flexible, 12s. 6d.

ANNANDALE'S CONCISE ENGLISH DICTIONARY. By Charles Annandale, M.A., LL.D. *New Edition, revised and extended*; 864 pp., f'cap 4to, cloth, 5s.; Roxburgh, 6s. 6d.; half-morocco, 9s.

A SMALLER ENGLISH DICTIONARY. Etymological, Pronouncing, and Explanatory. For the use of Schools. By John Ogilvie, LL.D. Cloth, 2s. 6d.; Roxburgh, 3s. 6d.

COMMON WORDS COMMONLY MISPRONOUNCED. With Hints on Correct Articulation. By W. Ramsay-Crawford. Cloth, 2s.

A PRONOUNCING VOCABULARY OF MODERN GEOGRAPHICAL NAMES, nearly ten thousand in number. By George G. Chisholm, M.A., B.Sc. F'cap 8vo, cloth, 1s. 6d.

New Series of Books for School Libraries and Prizes.

BLACKIE'S
SCHOOL AND HOME LIBRARY.

Carefully edited—clearly printed—strongly bound.

Under the above title the publishers have arranged to issue, for School Libraries and the Home Circle, a selection of the best and most interesting books in the English language.

In making a choice from the vast treasure-house of English literature the aim has been to select books that will appeal to young minds; books that are good as literature, stimulating, varied and attractive in subject-matter, and of perennial interest; books, indeed, which every boy and girl ought to know, and which, if once read, are sure to be read again and again.

The Library includes lives of heroes ancient and modern, records of travel and adventure by sea and land, fiction of the highest class, historical romances, books of natural history, and tales of domestic life.

NOW READY:

In crown 8vo volumes. Strongly bound in cloth. Price 1s. 4d. each.

The Rifle Rangers. By Captain Mayne Reid.
The Downfall of Napoleon. By Sir Walter Scott.
Essays on English History. By Lord Macaulay.
What Katy Did at School.
The Log-Book of a Midshipman.
Autobiographies of Boyhood.
Holiday House. By Catherine Sinclair.
Wreck of the "Wager" and Subsequent Adventures of her Crew.
What Katy Did. By Miss Coolidge.
Miss Austen's Northanger Abbey.
Miss Edgeworth's The Good Governess.
Martineau's Feats on the Fiord.
Marryat's Poor Jack.
Passages in the Life of a Galley-Slave.
The Snowstorm. By Mrs. Gore.
Life of Dampier.
The Cruise of the Midge. M. Scott.
Lives and Voyages of Drake and Cavendish.
Edgeworth's Moral Tales.

Irving's Conquest of Granada. 2 vols.
Marryat's The Settlers in Canada.
Scott's Ivanhoe. 2 vols.
Michael Scott's Tom Cringle's Log
Goldsmith's Vicar of Wakefield.
White's Natural History of Selborne
Cooper's The Pathfinder.
The Lamplighter. By Miss Cummins.
Old Curiosity Shop. 2 vols.
Plutarch's Lives of Greek Heroes.
Parry's Third Voyage.
Cooper's Deerslayer.
Miss Alcott's Little Women.
Marryat's Masterman Ready.
Scott's The Talisman.
The Basket of Flowers.
Miss Mitford's Our Village.
Marryat's Children of the New Forest.
Autobiography of Benjamin Franklin.
Lamb's Tales from Shakspeare.
Dana's Two Years Before the Mast.
Southey's Life of Nelson.
Waterton's Wanderings.
Anson's Voyage Round the World.

"The Library is one of the most intelligent enterprises in connection with juvenile literature of recent years. . . . A glance at the list proves that the editing is in the hands of some one who understands the likings of healthy boys and girls."—*Bookman.*

Detailed Prospectus and Press Opinions will be sent post free on Application.

LONDON: BLACKIE & SON, LIMITED; GLASGOW AND DUBLIN.

www.ingramcontent.com/pod-product-compliance
Lightning Source LLC
Chambersburg PA
CBHW030339170426
43202CB00010B/1173